MOUNTAIN WALK
versus
FORREST FENN

Also by Richard E. Saunier

*The Bottoms Up of International Development**

*Conservation of Biodiversity and the New Regional Planning**

Perspectives on Sustainable Development

*Dictionary & Introduction to Global Environmental Governance**

*With Dr. Richard A. Meganck

MOUNTAIN WALK
versus
FORREST FENN

a memoir

Richard E. Saunier

gatekeeper press™
Columbus, Ohio

The views and opinions expressed in this book are solely those of the author and do not reflect the views or opinions of Gatekeeper Press. Gatekeeper Press is not to be held responsible for and expressly disclaims responsibility of the content herein.

Mountain Walk versus Forrest Fenn: a memoir

Published by Gatekeeper Press
2167 Stringtown Rd, Suite 109
Columbus, OH 43123-2989
www.GatekeeperPress.com

Copyright © 2023 by Richard E. Saunier
All rights reserved. Neither this book, nor any parts within it may be sold or reproduced in any form or by any electronic or mechanical means, including information storage and retrieval systems, without permission in writing from the author. The only exception is by a reviewer, who may quote short excerpts in a review.

Library of Congress Control Number: t/k

ISBN (paperback): t/k
eISBN: t/k

For my brother, M. K. Saunier:
valued colleague and best friend.

He would have loved the chase.

Contents

Preface xi

Chapter 1   Why Am I Here?........................... 1

Chapter 2   Finding Forrest Fenn....................... 14

Chapter 3   Why Are You Here? 33

Chapter 4   Where Is It We're To Go? 63

Chapter 5   When Things Go South..................... 90

Chapter 6   Flotsam — No Charge 106

Chapter 7   A Penny For Your Thoughts 129

Chapter 8   Heroism................................ 140

Chapter 9   The Final Solve From Team Sleuthy-Guy 150

Bibliography 174

Acknowledgements................................... 179

As I have gone alone in there
And with my treasures bold,
I can keep my secret where,
And hint of riches new and old.

Begin it where warm waters halt
And take it in the canyon down,
Not far, but too far to walk.
Put in below the home of Brown.

From there it's no place for the meek,
The end is ever drawing nigh;
There'll be no paddle up your creek,
Just heavy loads and water high.

If you've been wise and found the blaze,
Look quickly down, your quest to cease,
But tarry scant with marvel gaze,
Just take the chest and go in peace.

So why is it that I must go
And leave my trove for all to seek?
The answers I already know,
I've done it tired, and now I'm weak.

So hear me all and listen good,
Your effort will be worth the cold.
If you are brave and in the wood
I give you title to the gold.

The Thrill of the Chase: a Memoir
by Forrest Fenn (2010)

Preface

In June of 2010 an event was held in Santa Fe, New Mexico to celebrate the release of a book by Forrest Fenn titled *The Thrill of the Chase: a Memoir (2010).* Having published at least a half dozen books before, he was no stranger to book signings. And, as beautifully done or historically valuable as they were, none of those books reached the audience or influence that this one did. The lives of thousands of people were changed because of his 2010 *Memoir*.

It starts slowly enough: a collection of short stories that relate to Forrest's time growing up in a small Texas town, his summers spent in and around Yellowstone National Park, his days as a pilot in Vietnam, a sentimental ode to his wife and daughters and his years as a business owner in Santa Fe.

Additional pieces include an essay on how and why he created and cast a series of bells that he buried around New Mexico and, then, a chapter that ensured that his *Memoir* would be the most studied of any book recently published. It has to do with a treasure chest he hid that held over a million dollars in gold and jewelry and his promise that anyone who found it could claim ownership.

To help guide this effort, his *Memoir* contains a poem with nine clues that tell how the treasure chest can be found (See opposite); other 'subtle' clues are supposedly scattered throughout the book.

With a few exceptions, the contents of *Mountain Walk versus Forrest Fenn* were first offered in the blog, *Mountain Walk* (wordpress), which was meant to help Fenn treasure hunters along in their attempts to locate and claim his treasure chest. You will find here 49 of the 64 posts written between early November, 2011 and late November, 2015. Those that escaped have gone off to a different project and are not at all relevant here.

To make a bit more sense of what I wrote, the 49 posts are ordered differently than they were in the blog. I took errors out, put notes in and tried to make the product read more like a book — with a beginning, a middle and an end. I have tried to maintain the conversational flavor of the blog throughout. Footnotes indicate the actual date of a blog posting.

Nine chapters are presented that generally begin with a story from my own experience meant to make an inference, a suggestion, or a rule on how to look for Forrest Fenn's treasure — or any other treasure for that matter — in the wildlands of the West.

The first posts announce the blog, put sideboards on how searches by Team Sleuthy-Guy[1] were to be made and then give, in more esoteric terms, the rationale behind a desire to search for anything and the pretext that it gives us to explore.

Then, eight posts highlight what we may want to know about Forrest Fenn, his personality, his character and his values. It just seems that we need to know this to justify our participation in a search for his treasure; such information may also help us find what we seek.

The next nine posts help to interpret the poem's clues, discuss other 'found' clues and suggest possible routes to the treasure.

Ten posts say what Team Sleuthy-Guy thought important for the search and include clues that appeared from out of nowhere that were used for 'paper' searches.

The next five posts look at the times the hunt went wrong and suggest ways to keep that kind of thing from happening. Searchers

---

[1] My team of supposed treasure hunters made up of family and friends.

often parachuted in from elsewhere and were unfamiliar with the nature of Nature in the West — that, or they had an enthusiasm that made their dreams far too large for the boney structure of Forrest's poetry to hold them aloft.

Innocence of this kind showed in very strange places and in very strange ways; ignoring rules and breaking laws hither and yon, the undisciplined of our fellow searchers left trails of ill-feelings, frayed friendships, damaged properties, and desecrated landmarks. Searchers went bankrupt, got divorced, lost friends or partners and some went to jail (Barbarisi, 2021).

Nor were they prepared mentally, physically or operationally for what they wanted to do. As a result, nine posts point to what it takes to be an explorer, an adventurer or a seeker of curious treasures.

An entire chapter is given over to a few selected comments made to *Mountain Walk* that represent the many others made over the life of the blog. Most notable was the comment of E. Jean Carroll, recently a writer for the glossy woman's magazine, Elle, who uses words like 'ravishing.' It's kind of like she wanted to bring a bit of needed culture to *Mountain Walk*.

I suspect that for every writer there is a difficult part of the project to write. They struggle with the concept no matter how real the subject before them. For me it was the deaths of treasure hunters and what that can mean to families left behind or for those who become entangled in the events though faultless. It seems that exaggerations and accusations color each of the incidents for no other reason than that, 'someone had to pay.' I apologize now to those who believe my arguments too raw or too simple. They are what they are and time and thought went into them. You don't have to believe them or even read them — they were meant for me.

The last chapter reports on the first 'solve' from Team Sleuthy-Guy made mid-August, 2012 and then summarizes a final, hypothetical solve now useless except that it shows where the treasure could have been hidden and may silence some of the naysayers. It may also add fodder for those who want to hang on to the chase just for the fun of it.

Richard E. Saunier
Tucson, Arizona
August 4, 2022

CHAPTER 1

Why Am I Here?

Why Am I Here? My wife and I moved back out West after five years of familial growth and social maturation in Latin America, 25 years of life in Maryland and too many years of work in Washington D. C. However, my beautiful wife would not entertain a move to my hometown of Española, New Mexico (she calls it the arm-pit of the State but I know she jests), so we built a home in Santa Fe.

A year or so later, friends who still lived in the East bought a small condo in Santa Fe and would schedule a visit two or three times a year or whenever they felt a need to be enchanted and each time they would also want to go on an 'adventure.'

So we adventured. But here 'adventure' should be written in a very small font because I was more of a tour guide for all things beautiful and interesting in Northern New Mexico than I was a Sherpa pulling super-rich novice climbers up Cabezon.[2]

We collected mushrooms at Ski Santa Fe; and took in the petroglyphs at Cieneguilla, Lyden and La Bajada; we investigated the ghost towns along the Rio Puerco and on the Llano Estacado. We visited the ancient churches at Chimayó, Cordova, Cuartelez,

---

[2] A well known, and easily seen, Devil's Tower-like volcanic plug in the Rio Puerco Valley of Northern New Mexico. Its peak rises straight up to 2000 feet above the valley floor (Ungande, 1965).

Arroyo Seco, Truchas and Las Trampas and walked over the ruins at San Gabriel. We hiked the Ghost Ranch and the Plaza Blanca and looked over the accouterments of a nuclear age collected by Ed Grothus at the 'Black Hole' in Los Alamos.[3]

I introduced them to the Indian potters at San Ildefonso, Santa Clara and San Juan; the Spanish wood carvers at Cordova and to the weavers at Truchas and Chimayó. We marveled at the energy and talent of Ra Paulette as shown in the cave he dug at Rancho de San Juan near Ojo Caliente. We photographed the bison at the Wind River Ranch just west of Watrous and visited with Ben C de Baca, the only resident of Loma Parda — a small ghost village in the middle of that ranch and once the site of the brothel for the soldiers at Ft. Union.

After a while, I was running short of available adventures though there were still many other places we should have gone — except we couldn't. The problem is that much of what was once open for an adventure is on private land with new owners and those adventures are no longer available.

I needed other places for show and tell close to Santa Fe and knew that Forrest Fenn owned San Lazaro, an abandoned Tono Pueblo southeast of the village of Cerrillos (Fenn, 2004). A neighbor to that ruin was a mutual friend so I asked her to introduce me to Mr. Fenn and she did.

We met for coffee and apple juice at the Collected Works Bookstore and before the coffee was gone and the apple juice finished, I had permission to visit the ruin and an unpaid, unrestricted and unexpected opportunity to write a blog about the chase for the treasure he had hidden away north of Santa Fe. That,

---

[3] I have included a Bibliography that includes publications that will introduce you to all of these sites.

in and of itself, sounded like an adventure. I said, "Yes" and named the blog *'Mountain Walk.'*

The first two or three years of the *Mountain Walk* blog were interesting and informative. I enjoyed the 'give and take' of the comments, and wrote what I thought was pretty good advice.

As time passed without the searchers even getting close to the treasure and as more and more of them clambered to get on board, things had gotten out-of-hand. Irate wannabe archeologists *cum* wannabe attorneys, and religious and 2nd Amendment trolls insisted that their nonsense be heard. Mercenaries attached themselves to the blog like remoras to a shark, and searchers began to argue over who had the real 'solve' though none but one of them ever found anything related to the treasure they absolutely knew was within their grasp. And that took ten years (Barbarisi, 2020).

The blog posts used here are most of those I wrote — all now useless for the purpose of finding Forrest's treasure. If nothing else, however, you may consider them as hints on how to survive an adventure in the West or, if so inclined, as essays that may or may not be good for the soul.

An additional piece outlines the final solve from Team Sleuthy-Guy. Of course, this final solve won't be any more successful than the others, but Team Sleuthy-Guy was always in it for the chase and not for the 'get.' Team members who are wiser than I, said the 'get' would most certainly cost more than it was worth and Mr. Stuef, the fellow who found the treasure in 2020, may soon find out if there is any truth in there.

Then came a six-year hiatus for *Mountain Walk* during which we sold our home and moved on to other things. But, since the treasure has been recovered and both Forrest and his bride, Peggy, are now at one with the Universe, the *Mountain Walk* blog likewise needs its final resting place and hopefully this book will be it.

And that is why I am here.

The World's Most Awesome Geocache:[4] For someone who barely knows how to open his e-mails, starting a blog is a foolhardy task at best. Who knows if I will ever find the thing again let alone change its design or add something new?

In any case, the purpose of this blog is to tell you how my search for the world's most awesome geocache is going and interpret clues along the way that may help you get off your duff so that you can go out there and find it yourself. Ostensibly, the cache is a treasure chest containing over $1,000,000 in gold and jewelry hidden by fellow Santa Fean, Forrest Fenn.

Others search for the treasure as well and some of them also have blogs that confess their failures to find the chest. But mostly those blogs are wonderful stories beautifully told about the discoveries their owners and guests make as they look for what they haven't yet found.

Mine will be a bit different in that I will try to explain the clues Forrest has given us in his memoir, *The Thrill of the Chase*, as I understand them. However, my thinking now is that I will do this with just enough of a time lag so that the best clues, the key, the final argument, will be known only to me until the treasure chest is safely locked away in my storage shed.

I will also try to be like Forrest and give just enough information to send you in the wrong direction even though the clue, if faithfully followed, could lead you in the right direction, down the correct valley, along a perfectly defined path to the exact spot where he may or may not have carefully placed his treasure.

You will have to do your part — especially if you want to get there before I do. First, to follow along or even jump ahead, you will need to buy the book, *The Thrill of the Chase, A Memoir* by Forrest Fenn that is available only from the Collected Works

---

[4] MntWlk Nov/02/2011

Bookstore in Santa Fe, New Mexico. Profits from the sales go to help pay for the treatment of children with cancer; how many children will depend upon you.

Second, you will have to forge ahead no matter how terribly bored you are with a post. I will try to keep each one at 750-1000 words so you won't stop reading and go elsewhere. Come back often and there will be something new although that depends on the snow conditions at Ski Santa Fe. I have reached the age where skiing is a 'freebie' so deadlines may not mean what they mean.

The book, *The Thrill of the Chase* itself, is filled with clues; probably more than Forrest intended and fewer than those I think I have found. I have divided all these clues into three buckets: 1) clues that will help us figure out just who Forrest Fenn is — a necessary task for a number of reasons. Of course, he will say that we make things up but pay no attention. He is much more open than he wants us to believe; 2) clues that will tell us whether or not it is true that he has hidden a fortune for anyone to find and possess — after the IRS has taken its share; and 3) my interpretation of real or imagined clues that will lead someone to the treasure.

I hope that you enjoy the chase and to get you off on the right foot, my first piece of advice is, "Don't put 'thrill of the chase' into your search engine." I tried that and the first six results were porn sites.

Intuition and the Art of Sleuthiness:[5] In addition to being a Fenn treasure blogger, I am also one of the amateurs who look for his treasure. Mr. Fenn has only recently discovered this although my wife had earlier told his wife, Peggy, that I not only look for the treasure, I have 'found' where it was hidden three times already but the treasure was never there. She also asked Mrs. Fenn to have Mr. Fenn declare the treasure 'recovered' before I spend all of our

---

[5] MtnWlk Nov/9/2011

retirement funds on equipment from REI and on overnight trips to nowhere. I must say that it has been a lot of fun so far.

The first post to this blog, suggested that you might want to follow my lead to find and interpret the clues of Forrest Fenn. Here, in the interest of staying out of legal trouble, I confess that the extent of my mystery-solving, puzzle-breaking training consists solely in a bit of unfinished half-hearted graduate work with *Colombo* in the mid-1990s and, earlier, undergraduate work with Agents, '86' and '99' of *Get Smart* in the 1960s. The first had a whole lot to do with an eye for detail, meticulousness and dedicated attempts to discover the meaning of even the most absurd of clues whereas Agents '86' and '99' trusted more in serendipity and dumb-luck for their solutions. Both, by which I mean serendipity and dumb-luck, will be needed if my search for Forrest Fenn's treasure is to be successful. This, I believe, is what so worries my wife and it is why you may want to follow your own advice instead.

A lack of trust not-with-standing, I have forged ahead and composed several self-imposed guidelines designed to keep my enthusiasm in check, ensure my utmost attention to detail, and, as I said, keep me out of jail. There are twenty of them and you may want to use them as well:

1. Find everything that is possible to know about Forrest Fenn; read everything he has written or that has been written about him.
2. To find the 'hidden' clues in *The Thrill of the Chase*, look for ambiguous or forced words or phrases or for unnecessary changes in detail. Find at least one 'clue' in each chapter no matter how far-fetched or improbable. You can cull them later.

3. Develop an exegesis of each of the known and suspected clues. Part two of this guideline is to find out what 'exegesis' means.
4. Develop interpretations to all clues in as much detail as possible.
5. Be aware of the possibility of blind alleys.
6. Do not discount anything that Forrest says is a 'clue.'
7. Authenticate any 'evidence' you think you may have discovered.
8. Interpretations of any clue must support interpretations of other clues — responses cannot be mutually exclusive.
9. Question anything not understood.
10. Do not make hasty conclusions. Try to disprove any conclusion felt to be the correct one; look for rival interpretations.
11. Search out related information or images elsewhere in any of the writings Forrest mentions or that you may think you have come across from other sources.
12. Question anything that appears as just a coincidence.
13. Do not automatically discount any clues no matter how absurd they may appear.
14. Check all key words in all clues against all definitions of those words.
15. Be aware that all nine clues from the poem in *Thrill of the Chase* are to be used and most should be followed in the order they occur in the poem.
16. The best explanation of the clues will be the one that responds to all of the clues especially if interpretations to clues found elsewhere backup the alternative chosen.
17. If you get tired of these guidelines or don't like them you can build your own set.
18. Though 'intuition' can often be wrong, it is not an enemy.

19. Explore. Whether it is inside or out-of-doors, if your heart is not beating as it did the first time you kissed your first beau or beauette, you're probably not going in a very interesting direction.
20. Which reminds me, don't go out alone and always, always take a whistle.

When Slugs Make Love:[6] A few years ago I stood on a deck closed in on three sides by white stucco walls about eight feet high. I stood there trying to figure out why humans, the most advanced species on earth — in all things, just could not seem to understand one another, to agree, to get along. I was after that one single thing that made the world go around, that made us what we are and that made us do what we do.

Having failed again, I was about to go back inside, when I noticed a slug of normal slug size peak over the wall and, at the same time, another slug appeared from under the deck beside that same barrier. They were separated by maybe ten feet on this clean, roughened wall of white stucco and they seemed to make a beeline for one another at a slug's pace and with all the riotous clamor that slugs are responsible for. It seemed as if nothing could slow them down. So I sat down to watch play out whatever it was that was about to play out.

As the two got nearer and nearer to one-another on this broad expansive field of play or of war, in my own mind, I began to hurry the story along. Was it really to be all-out war? A slugfest to beat all slugfests? Which one would I root for? Should I intervene and run the risk of throwing the workings of an entire ecosystem out of kilter? Granted it wasn't a pair of great bull elk squaring

---

[6] MtnWlk May/19/2012

off to keep, or to take, a harem but still, here before me was pure, raw nature!

When they got to within maybe an inch of one another they began to circle and then…they met and … embraced. I swear. They embraced and all their body parts began to visibly tingle. They wrapped each other in everything they had and truly, truly, physically became one. There was no separation at all; the single knot of being swelled to golf ball size but the color was not white. It was blue and gold and red and violet and it all glistened the glisten that only a fiery opal or a fresh abalone shell could ever equal.

Then, with only the tiniest bit of protoplasm attached, that single entity released from the wall and slowly lowered itself on a pale blue lanyard of its own tissue to hang motionless as if at rest.

After a minute or so, a small breeze caused the ball to touch the wall again, where it stayed. Slowly the color faded to sluggish brown, the one became two and they went their separate ways. I assume that names were exchanged.

Now… I wrote this for a couple of reasons. The first is because I wanted to share. After all, how many human lifetimes have passed without ever seeing slugs make love? I'm getting old and have been around the block more times than I want to remember. I mean, I have spent time on farms and ranches; my dad, brother and I raised any number of rabbits before I even got out of primary school; my wife and I have shared the same bed for over 60 years, and I have stayed in way too many thin-walled hotels.

But even now, I have to say that that incident there on a deck thirty-five or so years ago was one of the most sensuous and awe-inspiring that I had ever seen. It seemed that it was preformed especially for me; to make it abundantly clear that if I am to understand anything, it has to be through observation and not through the intellectual myopia of human arrogance.

Imagine if two people met like that. They would begin on opposite sides of a twenty-foot thick tower at a distance of over one and one half vertical football fields covered with hundreds of three-foot overhangs, meet without a word and undertake the most intimate act of any and all others. It also seemed to me to be the most perfect of communication — literally of communion.

That is the second reason I wrote the story down. I have mentioned the difficulties we will have to unravel all the things that Forrest Fenn taunts us with in his poetry, his photos, his stories, his clues, his metaphors, his 'blazes' and his life. The major difficulty, of course, is the temptation to move too fast, to 'get out ahead of our skis,' as the current crop of political commentators are want to say.

But, the folly of human conceit is large. The language of Forrest's *Memoir* is not my language. We will have to somehow think his thoughts and listen closely to what he has told us and not jump to conclusions. Anything less would be foolish — even dangerous, and a totally useless method for finding his treasure.

Intuition:[7] My wife can walk up to any dog, anywhere, and say, "Hi Sweetie," stick out her hand and after a sniff or two, scratch it behind the ears. Dogs just seem to know.

If she sees a cat, she says, "Hi, Sweetie," and in five-seconds, the cat is on her lap being scratched under the chin. Cats just seem to know.

The first time I saw her, from thirty yards away without knowing if she were married, engaged, or otherwise compromised, I just seemed to know that my single days were over and that was over 60 years ago.

It shouldn't have happened, of course. I had years of school ahead of me and I had no money. There were things I wanted to

---

[7] MtnWlk Aug/2/2014

do, places I wanted to see, and there were friendships that would not let go. And yet I knew.

Five years later, after finishing a long stretch of graduate work, we were invited to Chile. In many ways, it meant the postponement of a career that I had planned for since the age of thirteen. It meant a new culture, a new language and new challenges. On this side, there were aging parents and promises made. And yet, we knew.

It is a marvelous thing, this thing that evolution has given us. Certainly intuition is often at odds with reason, its younger sibling, but that is only because we let it happen. When we use the part of our brain responsible for reason, our reply is slow. We need data, we need analysis, we need conversation and we need time. Further, there appear to be a number of cells and synapses that continuously jump in front of the reason train to slow things down even more.

Intuition is different. It resides in a different place and is variously described as 'instinct,' a 'sixth sense,' a 'gut feeling,' a 'tug at the heart.' But if you take any of these descriptors and break them apart you will find that they are the result of millions of individual bits of information gathered by all of our senses throughout our personal histories that are then stored in the corners of our mind, in our subconscious, to be called upon when needed — even when we don't realize they are needed.

And that is why I put number 18 in my list of 20 things to be aware of while we search for Forrest Fenn's treasure (*Intuition and the Art of Sleuthiness*). It says, "Intuition is not an enemy." But neither is it a guess. Learn the difference.

Coincidence?[8] So, intuition may not be an enemy; but what about coincidences?

---

[8] MtnWlk Nov/27/2014

More than a while ago, I left the United States mid-winter for Brazil. I thought I had packed just right for the temperature there but, it turned out, I was several degrees short. As a result, on one of our long lunch breaks, I went off to find a new shirt and bought one that was kind of splotchy with light blue and light tan and light white splotches; it made me look very Brazilian.

A couple of years later I was in a hotel dining-room in Amman, Jordan having a normal Jordanian hotel breakfast while I pretended to be a Brazilian when I looked up from my yoghurt and two olives to see a fellow on the other side of the room with the exact same shirt as the one I had on; same blue, tan and white splotches with the same elegant Brazilian cut. Was it just a 'coincidence' or was it a Soviet spy playing with my head?

One of my now aging nephews went by Cairo, Egypt a year or so after his college graduation to see his parents before he went off to count refugees from the Vietnam War. While in Cairo he decided that he really had to climb a pyramid — the big one — just to see if he could.

So, one dark night, as he neared the apex of his climb, he heard voices. He got to the summit and there, seated on that small space, was a young couple half of which was a high-school classmate who may or may not have been an ex-girlfriend. Was it just a 'coincidence'? Or was it a 'payback' she had conjured up say… six years earlier?

I have a friend from the old Chile days that I have seen maybe five times in the last 45 years — all of them by chance in places like a street in Mexico City, a restaurant in Guatemala, a hotel in Quito and, once, in the men's room in the San Jose, Costa Rica airport where, while I was just standing there staring at the wall, a fellow slides in beside me and starts to prattle away about a subject that seemed familiar. It was his final point to a discussion we had five years earlier.

Why Am I Here?

The web machine is full of people who want to figure out just what a coincidence actually is. As far as I can tell, they come in three kinds, by which I mean the people.

There are the mathematicians-statisticians, who, after many, many pages of very dense statistical stuff normally found only in my nightmares, who conclude that there is one chance in a gazillion billion that they will ever get it right.

There is the 'God group' whose answer is immediate and with absolute certainty that it is their 'Friend on High' who had it all planned out a few thousand years ago (but this only works for the things that make us feel good).

And then there is the third group made up of even more confident folk who say that, "There ain't no such thing as a 'coincidence,' no matter how much something may look like one."

I normally fall in one or the other of the three groups depending on the latest made-up conspiracy theory from *Infowars* and whether or not my lovely wife has made us a sandwich of yoghurt, and cucumber salad stuffed into pita bread along with all the olives I can eat.

Now, to put all of this into the context of why you are wasting your time reading it, I know of a small lake somewhere north of Santa Fe that I am absolutely almost certain that Forrest Fenn also knows, and the name of that lake is the same as that of a clan of Forrest Fenn's not so long-lost relatives.

"Coincidence," you say? I doubt that's what it is because what you are really doing is wondering just where on earth that lake may be.

Fine. But I'm wondering what happened to that splotchy shirt. And what troubles most is that I'll surely find it long before any of us find Forrest Fenn's treasure.

CHAPTER 2

Finding Forrest Fenn

For many reasons, we need to find all we can about Forrest Fenn. These next nine posts say who I thought he was in terms of personality, intelligence, values, interests, experiences, travels and sensibilities. Did I do it? Only he knows and he ain't gonna tell.

A Wannabe Saint:[9] A need to find everything we can about the 'perpetrator' of a mystery — in this case, Forrest Fenn, terrifies because there is no telling what you will find when you try to get close to the real Forrest Fenn; to fill in a few more details of his life history; to discover his habits, worries, and preferences; to know his friends and his enemies; to see his allegiances and followers; to follow his travels and fathom his likes and dislikes. But I will tell you anyway.

The easy part of this exercise, of course, was his date of birth (August 22,1930). "Why is that important?" some youngster will ask. Its important because that birthdate gave him 80 years on this earth when he secreted away a fortune for us to find. It is probably the single most important piece of information a searcher should know and the second most important is that at the age of 58 he was diagnosed with cancer. A third piece of information — more or less easy to find because it is in his *Memoir* — is that he knew

---

[9] MtnWlk Feb/28/2012

a lot of famous people like Jackie Kennedy, Susanne Somers, and Leslie Wray McBride.

Something a bit more difficult to find was that Forrest Fenn was raised a Southern Baptist with a trace of Mormonism he picked up from somewhere. Now that you know this, I want you to also know that the above statement is a declaration and not, as some would suggest, an accusation.

Still, it was an easy sleuth. The funeral for his father was held at the First Baptist Church in Temple, Texas and attended by an overflow crowd. A Web search of that church told me that it has pretty much always been allied with Southern Baptists. And, since we know that the young Forrest Fenn would show up at 'church socials,' we know that the Fenn family was at least somewhat familiar with the affairs of that church. That tells me of the relentless, near ruthless pressure that Forrest had as a kid to become a member of the First Baptist Church of Temple, Texas.

My interpretation of this information was also relatively easy. It helped that my father and father-in-law were deacons; my brother a minister; my wife a seminarian; and I, an excommunicate from Southern Baptist churches.

Now you ask, "Other than being interesting in a voyeuristic sort of way, does this information tell us anything? Does it get us any closer to the treasure?" Of course it does and maybe I will get to it later — much, much later.

What will also come later but not from me, is the other side of Forrest Fenn — the dark side. I haven't yet seen it in Forrest but I know it is there. All of us have one — some darker than others, deeper than others or thicker than others, and some have more than one. If and when I find Forrest's, I won't tell and if you find it just remember that old adage about throwing stones.

But for now I want to begin with an interesting obsession of Southern Baptists. That is, all good Southern Baptists leave the comfort of their homes for a hard wooden pew to listen to some 170 sermons a year, and all of this sermonizing is, supposedly, based on something called 'exegesis' (Rule #3, *Intuition and the Art of Sleuthiness*).

A very simple and somewhat erroneous definition of 'exegesis' is that it is 'parsing' which, I have learned, has nothing to do with gourmet cooking. Parsing is what journalists did several years ago to fathom the meanderings of the then Governor of Alaska. They had to identify the verb(s), object(s) and a bunch of modifiers in her statements, put them in an intelligible order and then figure out why a whole new topic would suddenly appear in the middle of it all. To parse, one needs only to be a very, very patient grammarian.

'Exegesis' is something else. It's what scholars do when they try to prove one another wrong as they argue over the interpretation of ancient, often sacred, texts. It involves an understanding of the cultural *milieu* within which the text was written; it looks at the text's provenance and chain of custody and the nuances of its original language. It attempts to identify the author or authors through an analysis of the writing styles and supposed personalities of the writer(s); it looks at the various meanings of each word; and it considers the people for whom and for what purpose it was written. With some adaptation, this is what we will have to do with each of Forrest Fenn's clues.

For example, take what is perhaps the very first clue in his *Memoir* and one I have mentioned before:

> I tend to use some words that aren't in the dictionary, and others that are; I bend a little. (Page 3, *Thrill of the Chase*).

This sentence was not written for the casual reader; it was written for us — the ones who look for his treasure. It is there to warn us to be careful when we decipher other of his clues because things could be 'fudged' and that no matter what we think we know about a clue, we could easily be somewhat off and that difference will be the difference between success and total frustration.

It's a fair warning that comes from Forrest Fenn himself.

The Man, the Myth, and the Mercer:[10] Anyone who watched *Colombo* for more then two shows knows that the development of a profile of the perpetrator is a key to solving a mystery. This is a short profile of the perpetrator of our little mystery, Forrest Fenn.

If you have read Forrest's memoir, *The Thrill of the Chase*, you know that he is the former owner of a very successful art gallery in Santa Fe, New Mexico as well as a writer of books, a philanthropist, an amateur archeologist of note and a collector of many things — gold, knives, books, art, bottle caps and bits of string. Mostly, though, he collects the artifacts of early North American Indians of the Plains and the Rockies. He is a fly fisherman and a lover of all things mountains — specifically the greater Yellowstone ecosystem.

He is a pilot, a veteran of two wars, a risk-taker and a decorated hero; a ruggedly built gentleman with a friendly face and an immense curiosity. He has the imagination of a five-year old steadied with the discipline of a warrior. Other than a small number of National Park retirees, he is one of the few people who now live in New Mexico who actually know who Osborne Russell was.

I am fairly sure that no one ever called Forrest Fenn dumb — except for Forrest himself, a couple of 'old biddies' from his youth, his teenage chum, Donnie Joe, and maybe his Spanish teacher. To be sure, his own statements say that he slept through classes, barely made it out of high school and, overcome by a fit of what

---

[10] MtnWlk Nov/17/2011

some would call foolhardiness, he is now offering up a million dollars for the taking.

On the other hand, he also flew close to 300 combat missions in one of the most complicated fighting machines ever built and, for a time, held a nuclear weapon in his care. He made a fortune in a very competitive business where he had no formal education or prior experience and then published half a dozen books on the subject. A diagnosis of ADHD has got to be in his files somewhere.

Consequently, when Forrest makes light of his education and mental faculties, he uses his considerable native intelligence to lull you to sleep, to win you over and then give you a thorough trouncing. Despite his being tossed from an unregistered space at Texas A&M and being twice shot out of the SouthEast Asian sky, I am guessing that Forrest has seldom been defeated at something he really wanted to win.

Forrest has a crafty side to him. His admitted sales philosophy is that of a game that he will win, not by cheating but by setting you up. Some of his anecdotes in *The Thrill of the Chase* are examples of such behavior. He even offers a few oblique phrases in the very first chapters that explain what he is up to:

Occasionally it's wise for the fox to dress like the hound (p. 7),

I never thought I had to believe every thing I said (p. 14) and,

later, in a story called 'Jump-starting the Learning Curve,' his father councils,

What we have learned is that you should always tell the truth, but you should not always tell ALL of the truth (p. 26).

Thus, among the clues that he has given us, one must fully expect 'clues' that are not what they seem at first reading. Perhaps one of the best clues in the entire book is one of these. On p. 131 he writes,

> I knew exactly where to hide the chest so it would be difficult to find but not impossible. It's in the mountains somewhere north of Santa Fe.

Note the difference between that sentence and,

> ...a treasure chest he says he *buried somewhere in the mountains north of Santa Fe.*

And therein lies the trap. All news articles I have seen on the subject of his treasure chest interpret their own rephrasing of his statement to mean,

> ...Buried in the mountains of Northern New Mexico.

That, however, is not what Forrest Fenn said. His statement could mean that he hid his treasure in any of the mountains from Santa Fe north to, and through, Alaska.

Likewise, he never says that he 'buried' the treasure but only that he 'hid' it. The Nation's press from *The Santa Fe New Mexican* to *The New York Times* have conspired to lead us astray and I am convinced a chuckle can be heard every time Forrest reads such things.

Despite this discovery after a detailed analysis of his profile, I am not sure if this bit of information helps a whole lot. Before, we had to look in what amounted to two National Forests, a couple of areas managed by the National Park Service and several square miles belonging to the Bureau of Land Management. Now we have over a hundred national parks and forests covering several million acres that we have to think about.

The Naysayers:[11] I couldn't help but notice the naysayers who read and comment on the blogs and the many articles that describe Forrest Fenn's treasure hunt. They are the doubters, skeptics and cynics who believe that Forrest is pulling our collective leg; that he has decided, as one of his last formal, public acts, to play us for fools rather than do what he says he has done — that is, to offer up a million dollar treasure to those who would decipher his clues and go out looking.

I am somewhat torn by this bit of information. On the one hand, it means that fewer people will search for his treasure. And, on the other, it could also mean that we as a people have 'developed' to where the kind of challenges offered by Forrest are seen as meaningless amusement and that wilderness no longer draws us from our comforts as it once did.

It means that the heroic/tragic tales of Meriwether Lewis, William Clark, and Sacagawea, of Joe Meek and Tom Fitzpatrick, of Kit Carson and of Jim Bridger now molder unread in forgotten libraries and that we have lost something special.

There is no need to question or to defend the honesty of Forrest Fenn. We need only to look at his motives and see what they say and, fortunately, *The Thrill of the Chase* has more clues about this part of Forrest than it has about how to find the treasure. In short, despite a far above average biography, Forrest fears to leave this world as unknown and unremembered and the rediscovery of the life of Forrest Fenn in a hundred or a thousand years would be his ideal scenario.

---

[11] MtnWlk Nov/25/2011

We know this because he left a number of 20,000-word autobiographies in the bronze jars and bells he fabricated and hid around New Mexico and he fantasizes about his desire to be buried along side his treasure chest. He is saddened that the name of his father appears but once in a Web search along with the number of his burial plot in a small Texas town. He writes poignantly of a late night solo flight down the East Coast as he ruminates on our place in the Universe. He brings tears with an account of his accidental encounter with the grave of a French soldier in Vietnam who, without Maj. Fenn's intervention, would have gone through eternity with no one to remember who he was, nor how and where he died.

I have the same fears as Forrest Fenn; we all do. No matter what we profess to believe, what we know for sure is that we will die and what will be left is our legacy and nothing more. For most of us, even that will soon fade away. Few of the billions of individual stories that have played out here on Earth attain the lasting levels of fame reached by Moses, Madam Curie or King Tutankhamen.

But we are all somebody. Our determination to hang on to that living uniqueness — even in death — is as strong as our desires for a great many other things — like, for example, a king's ransom in gold and jewelry. For me, it would be difficult not to believe that Forrest Fenn's treasure chest is hidden out there somewhere.

Maybe though, the naysayers need a more practical answer as to why they should trust Forrest Fenn on this one. Let me provide that answer. Much of Forrest's fortune obviously is in gold and jewelry rather than in Wall Street investments. What difference does it make then, if a part of his gold and jewelry is under his bed or hidden somewhere where he has every confidence that it will not soon be discovered?

The Cartographer:[12] I want you to know that I have looked at Forrest's map on page 133 of *The Thrill of the Chase* (Figure 1) for what seems like days, weeks, months on end. Not that that is all bad, mind you. I love maps — even when they are of places I have never been nor where, unfortunately, I will never go.

Figure 1: 'THE MAP.' *The Thrill of the Chase.*

Maps help conjure up all kinds of great adventure stories and, in North America, the best ones to do that are the old antique maps made by those sometimes skilled, often self-taught cartographers of the early years of Manifest Destiny; of Lewis and Clark and the mapmakers who dutifully put to paper the names, words and places traveled by the mountain men, who, whether French, Spanish or Irish, had a way of describing the essence of a landscape that is lost on no-one.

---

[12] MtnWlk Dec/22/2011

From *Tetilla* peak (Spanish) that I can see from my office window, to *les Trois Tétons* (French) of western Wyoming to . . . well, I don't need to tell you about the Irish. You understand what I mean. These early travelers never lacked for realistic descriptions nor did they suffer a loss of imagination; and their vocabularies were very much those of uncommon common men.

But do I care for new, modern maps? Not so much. They all seem to be about ranches or farms sold to developers just so they could undo the ancient trails and traces — the very names of which tell of hardships and successes won only with great difficulty — and then saddle them with names like 'Lily Lane' or 'Hibiscus.'

Now the falls, cataracts and steep narrow canyons that were always dangerous encounters for those early travelers are hidden by reservoirs and diversions that have destroyed the very personalities of rivers that for many hundreds of thousands of years molded the landscapes of which they are a part.

What have I found in Forrest Fenn's map after all this blinking and thinking? Well, for one, it's just about the fuzziest map I ever saw, and it makes me dizzy, and it doesn't help matters when I use a magnifying glass.

After a couple of months of eye-blinking and brow-mopping over THE MAP, as it has come to be called in our house, an epiphany of sorts occurred right there in front of me while I re-read Forrest's wonderful story about how he let children touch the nose of George Washington in a very expensive painting of that very same George Washington, when one of the young ladies discovered that that George Washington was the *reverse* of the George Washington she had in her pocket!

I've no doubt that many of you have looked at that MAP for hours just like me. It made you dizzy and you used a magnifying glass. But how many of you have scanned that MAP and then put it in Photoshop so that you could reverse and then sharpen it?

Aha! And now you want *me* to tell *you* what I discovered? Well, here it is and it won't cost you a percentage of the take if you find the treasure because of it.

What I found was that if you scan THE MAP and then reverse it in Photoshop and then sharpen it, you have an image that resembles pretty much every mountain range and river in the United States west of Arkansas.

Captain Kidd:[13] Last spring my favorite daughter-in-law brought our then one year-old grandson out to see us. Yes, I understand that this is a blog meant to tell just how to find the exact spot where Forrest left his treasure chest in 2010 and I will do that, but I figure that a few words about my grandson might also be in order; I am, after-all, a new grandfather.

A remarkable little kid he is. For example, whenever he tired of trying to convince me in English that he absolutely had to have another cookie, he resorted to ASL (American Sign Language) thinking, no doubt, that the battery must have gone dead in my hearing aid.

I will give a whole lot more detail on his numerous achievements as well as his suggestions as to how we should interpret the clues of Forrest Fenn in later posts. This one, however, is about how he influenced the discovery of the secrets hidden in THE MAP.

When we met the two of them (favorite daughter-in-law and grandson) at the airport in Albuquerque the day they arrived, my daughter-in-law asked me how I was doing. I said, "Fine. I'm going to be a millionaire just as soon as I decipher THE MAP from Forrest Fenn's memoir, *The Thrill of the Chase*."

---

[13] MtnWlK Jan/2/2012

Her response, as I remember it, was something like, "Yeah. Right." Then, she slowly shook her head, turned away, hugged my wife and handed her our grandson.

I sat in the rear seat on the way back to Santa Fe from Albuquerque just so I could quiz my grandson on whether or not he understood anything that a certain reality show personage had ever said, but as we left the garage my daughter-in-law offered him her I-Pad which he took and, even before we reached the garage pay-booth, he had the I-Pad opened and turned on; had selected what appeared to be his very own file, and was debating whether he should watch 'Curious George meets Allie Oops' or something called 'Bunny Hunt' which, as far as I could tell, had absolutely nothing to do with Hugh Hefner, *Playboy*, or the NRA.

Given that I had now been replaced by something I knew nothing about, a nap seemed appropriate. The trip home, therefore, was uneventful except from time to time my grandson would poke me, point to the monitor, look me in the eye as if he knew something I didn't and say what sounded very much like *'Apsáalooke pwat'* whereupon I would nod, take his word for it, and go back to sleep.

On our arrival home, I asked my daughter-in-law if she wanted to see THE MAP. Her response, as I remember it, was something like, "What map?"

I once again explained that, "I was about to be a millionaire just as soon as I deciphered THE MAP" and she asked me what the problem was. "It makes me dizzy," I answered.

So we went to my desk in the office where I shoved aside three or four loupes of various magnifications, wiped a spot of spaghetti sauce off the page opposite THE MAP and showed it to her (by which I mean THE MAP, not the sauce).

She took the book, opened it to page 133, held it at oh, about 15 inches in front of her nose for all of 12 seconds, handed it back to me, knelt down to grab hold of the diaper my grandson was wearing to keep him from the brownish colored apple-core that had sat beside my wastebasket for all of a week and said, "It's a map of Northern New Mexico."

Incredulous, I stood there, looked at THE MAP (Figure 1, page 25.) for the two-hundred-forty-second time, squinted my eyes and, sure enough, it was.

Then, as she dashed out the office door to grab my now diaper-less grandson in an unsuccessful attempt to keep him from pouring more cat food into the cat's water bowl, she added, "And there is a Captain Kidd-like pirate 'X' about an inch and a quarter above the top gold nugget."

And, sure enough, there was.[14]

Land Surveyor:[15] The most complicated and inherently tenacious problem in large parts of the Globe is the question of 'who owns what piece of real estate.' University departments have been founded just to find its solutions; hundreds of western movies have been filmed with that very problem as their theme; and, more importantly, it causes far too many wars.

Yet, at the local level, responses can often be both practical and precise. For example, a Peruvian extension agent who attended a Dutch conference on the subject was asked how he solved the problem — how he knew which parcel of land belonged to which farmer. The agent answered simply that when a different dog barks he knows that he has crossed from the property of one owner to the property of another.

This is not how the early folk in our country divided up the lands previously settled by even earlier folk who couldn't solve

---

[14] Actually, there are at least three of them — none more important than the others.
[15] MtnWlk Apr/16/2012

the problem either. What our forefathers did was declare a clean slate with no land ownership but by the government and then let those who could work the land mark off a chunk and legally claim it as their own. The way the piece of land was officially described by the surveyor was by use of something called 'Metes and Bounds.'

Osbourne Russell — a favorite mountain man of Forrest's — after he lost an eye (Osbourne Russell I mean), decided to become a farmer and on October 23,1845, he recorded a land claim in Oregon Territory. The description by the land surveyor says the following (Haines, 1955):

> ... situate and beginning at a fir tree 3 feet in Diameter, standing 800 yards south west of the falls of the north branch of the Lukamyute River, and blazed on the north and east sides, thence running north 600 yards to the stream, thence crossing said stream and running north 1130 yards to three Oaks each 6 inches Diam — standing together on the side of the Mountain, one blazed on the south and another on the east side — thence running nearly east one mile, to an oak tree two feet in Diam — blazed on the west and south sides, standing on a high ridge — thence south 1200 yds to the stream, thence crossing the stream and running nearly south 560 yds to an Oak tree 12 inches Diam standing on the side of a ridge, and blazed on the north & west sides — thence west to the place of beginning.

You get the idea. These were the 'metes.' You start at a certain point, face a given direction, go a certain distance, face a different direction, go a certain distance, etc. until you hit the point where you started. It has to do with direction and distance from a known feature like the falls of the North branch of the Lukamyute River' or, more to the point, 'Begin it where warm waters halt.'

In addition, a land claim was described by 'bounds,' that is, by the appearance and tenure of the landscape that surrounds the land claim. In Osborne Russell's case:

> ...said claim is bounded on the west by Mountainous forest, on the north by a high spur of Mountain, which divides the waters of the Lukamyute and LeCreole rivers, on the east, north of the stream, by a tract of Prairie Land supposed to be claimed, by Chas Eaten — south of the stream by a tract of prairie claimed and occupied by Adam Brown and on the south by vacant ridgy Land, and spurs of Mountain.

Now, there is no reason that the piece of land being defined must be 640 acres or 160 acres or 80 acres. It could be six square feet—a piece of land just the right size to hide a brass box 10" x 10" x 6" full of gold and jewelry; the system of 'metes and bounds' would still work. And a method of 'direction and distance' from a given point would work equally well to take one to that very same six square feet piece of land in the first place.

Anyone who has ever filed a flight plan knows the rudiments of metes and bounds even if it is not called that. And Forrest Fenn has filed thousands of flight plans. Did he use some form of metes and bounds to give us clues as to where he hid his treasure? I think so...but he did it in an obscure language called 'poetry' and in old photographs and other vague imagery. So, between the poem and the other clues hidden in his *Memoir*, distances and directions are there and a description of the surrounding landscape is there — but all of it is masked by symbol and metaphor.

I wrote this post to explain how people in the old days used direction and distance to locate and mark off bits of land on a much larger landscape and not to suggest that we go looking for Forrest Fenn's treasure with an early visit to the old homestead of Osbourne Russell and his neighbor to the South — Mr. Brown.

Head Fakes:[16] It's March and everybody knows what that means. Is it that I am a year older? I am, but that is not it. Is it the month that Julius Caesar died? It is, but that's not it either.

No, this is the month that my lovely wife commandeers the TV remote because it is the time of the year for 'March Madness'— that part of early spring when the 68 best college basketball teams in the country, each with a couple of seven foot tall players from Eastern Europe plus Spain and a shooting guard from Canada, are whittled down to 60 + 8 teams on the outer edge that must 'play in' to give 64 and then to 32 and then 16, then eight, then four and then to two and then, at last, to one.

That last team will be the one that has the best discipline, the best conditioning, the best strategies, the best talent, the best teamwork and the best motivation and all of that together guarantees two things: one, a really heavy trophy and two, at least half of that team's players will soon become instant NBA millionaires.

If you are keeping track, all that besting comes out to be something like exactly 67 games played over a three week period all of it filled with head fakes, slam-dunks, ally-oops, lay-ups, turn-overs, three-pointers, rebounds, fouls, flips, slips, missed free-throws, more missed free-throws (I'm talking Arizona here), overtimes, upsets and tears from grown men.

You are now thinking that my wife hides the remote so that I can get the breakfast dishes done with time left over to work on

---

[16] MtnWlk Mar/24/2014

the income tax before it's soon to arrive deadline but you would be wrong.

Not only did she finish the income tax last January, the dishes are put away before I even get to the daily Sudoku. More importantly, my beautiful wife was a college cheerleader back when they wore anklets, mid-calf skirts and had chaperones. But did she just sit there in her little uniform with pleats, yell 'Yea' from time to time and smack the palms of her hands on the floor every now and then in a strange rhythm known only to cheerleaders and rock drummers? No! She soaked up every strategy, every nuance, and every rule of the game and now she is a FAN and that, as you know, is short for 'FANATIC!' She is such a fanatic that she knows the difference between a 'high-post' and a 'low-post,' and not only does she know what 'RPI' stands for, she can calculate it as well as tell you the hometown of Gonzaga.

But that is not why I am here. I am here to tell you of my discovery that Forrest Fenn is a champion 'head faker' himself; perhaps the best head faker of all head fakers –- even those from Duke, and we fall for them all.

Now, a head fake is not lying; it's more like a little hint at something that might be true in the aggregate but means nothing in the specific.

We will need a whole lot of discipline and all that other stuff if we are to let the head fakes of Forrest Fenn slide by and not end up face down on the floor with a sprained ankle.

Edie:[17] It's spring-cleaning time at our house. Of course, it's not really spring and most people not my wife cringe at the thought of starting it early; but this one has turned into something special. We keep finding notes from Edie.

---

[17] MtnWlk Mar/1/2014

Edie came by to see us last November. She is the granddaughter of some old, old friends and the last time I saw Edie's mother she was about ten and showing off some really smooth ballerina moves and now she has a family of her own. They were driving across the country heading home and spent a couple of days with us.

Edie is four going on forty-five and from the looks of it she and her red cowboy boots are inseparable. The morning after a late night arrival she was in the kitchen. I said, "Hi, I'm Richard" and she said, "Hi, I'm Edie" and shook my hand.

Edie collects rocks so I dug out my collection of the thumb-size shiny ones I've collected from every place I have ever been for her to check out. She went through them all, looking over each one and then put them back in the gourd I store them in.

Ellery, her younger brother, age one, also wanted to see them. He carefully took them out of the gourd, tasted each one, and set them aside. Edie put them back when he was through with his taste test.

Collecting rocks is about as good a hobby as a body can have (Baylor, 1985). Each one carries with it the memory of a place and a time and it is an inexpensive thing to do except when you start hauling them around the country. Problem is that we are at the age where we are thinking about 'down-sizing' as well as 'spring-cleaning' and the only things I really want to keep are my rocks. My wife prefers her coffee pot thingies so a day of reckoning fast approaches.

I try to convince myself that collecting rocks is as good as keeping a journal but I secretly know that not keeping a journal is one of my great failings. Of course, a taste test does help with that memory thing but I hope that Edie and Ellery keep a journal and that they start when they get to be, say, about twelve.

Edie also likes to play 'hide and seek' but it's not the game we played when we were kids. Like someone else I know who collects everything from bottle caps to gold, she enjoys hiding things that everyone else has to find. So Edie and her mother wrote out just about everything Edie likes on little pieces of paper and then she made us all close our eyes as she hid them just so we could learn about something called 'thrill of the chase.' Each find brought a smile and a giggle to Edie. Now we find the really well hidden ones during spring-cleaning, and we smile, and it makes moving furniture something special.

When they were leaving I gave Edie a rock with a fossil in it. I said, "Bye Edie" and she said, "Bye" and then I got a hug. It was a treasure worth waiting for.

So I've been thinking. Forrest Fenn, with his habit of collecting things and then hiding them for others to find is in very, very good company — and the world is a better place because of it.

I think he knows that.

CHAPTER 3

Why are You Here?

Now that is a good question. Why in the world are you here? I mean, Forrest Fenn's treasure chest has been found; his treasure hunt is over.[18]

Really?

Yes, the gold, jewels and a valuable old box have been found, inventoried, and stored away in some lawyer's office vault. But if I recall correctly, and I do, those showy items were only part of the treasure Forrest wanted us to search for, that he wanted us to chase after, and to do our best to find. There were treasures out there far beyond the box and its contents that he also wanted us to know. He wanted us to experience the chase for all kinds of treasures, to feel the thrill of it, and to believe in the ubiquity of it. The search was to be continued for as long as we, the searchers, were able. And maybe, just maybe, that is why you are here.

We know that for Forrest, the treasures were the out-of-doors, his books, and his desire to find and to feel the life that remained in antiquities. He wanted to understand the West and its history; he sought out special kinds of art and was friends with one-of-a-kind artists. And he then wrote books about all of it because he wanted us to participate in the things he thought deserved our attention, our interest and our respect (Fenn, 2010).

---

[18] The chest was found in June of 2020 in Wyoming by Jack Stuef.

Forrest Fenn to Star in Remake of Blazing Saddles:[19] I am seldom asked anything anymore except by my grandson who is always asking for another cookie. He knows more than I do, of course; it's just that he can't reach the cookie jar so the old guy is still of some use. Besides, it's one of those win-win things since I also always need another cookie.

Nevertheless, I *am* sometimes queried by individuals who believe themselves treasure hunters. Two of their questions stand out: "You've found it already, haven't you?" or more often, "Just where are you looking?"

There is another question regarding Forrest's treasure that I overheard so it doesn't really count as someone seeking my advice even though I do know the answer. I have delayed giving it out because to do so could say far too much. I only do it now because...well, once again, I know you will share the treasure with me if you find it. The question is, "What's a blaze?"

First, before we get to say what a blaze is, we should mention what it isn't. That is, a blaze is not graffiti though some graffiti may be significant and go a long way toward proving that you stand near a spot where someone else once stood. If that person is of interest to you then it seems that that bit of graffiti can count as a 'blaze.'

The 'graffiti' at El Morro National Monument in New Mexico (Figure 2), for example, consist of a large number of blazes if you are interested in things like Juan de Oñate's excursions about the Southwest; and it would have been especially so if you were a part of his party but for some reason found yourself trailing behind on the return to San Juan Pueblo from his 'discovery' of the 'Sea of the South.'

---

[19] MtnWlk Jun/5/2012

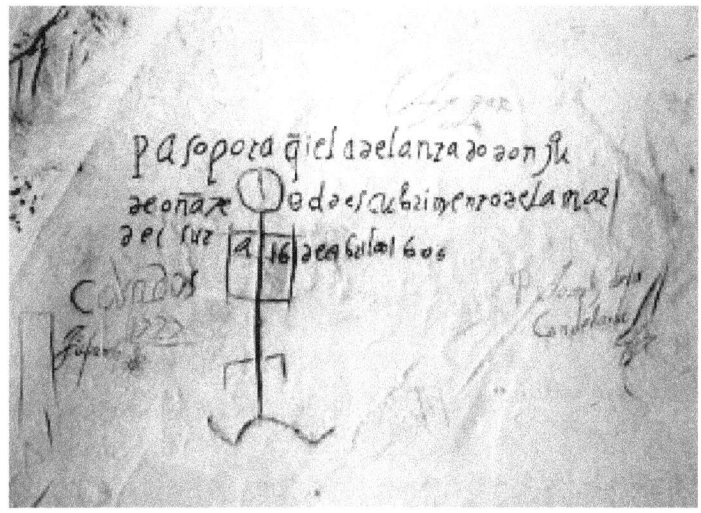

Figure 2: Oñate 'graffiti,' El Morro National Monument, New Mexico. *(Paso por aqui, el adelantado Don Juan de Oñate del descubriamiento de la mar del sur a 16 de Abril de 1605)*[20]

Second, there are all kinds of blazes — the white mark on a horse's nose and forehead; the metaphoric successful first pass or attempt towards anything; the emblem near the breast pocket of the sport coat called, incidentally, a 'blazer;' Usain Bolt's lightening fast speed in the 100 and 200 meter races; the final scenes of *Butch Cassidy and the Sundance Kid* in which they go down in a 'blaze of glory'; a fire, a lightning strike, a meteor arcing across the sky; trail markers made with any color of paint, surveyor's tape, metal or plastic disks; a patch cut out of a tree's bark; rocks, sticks, or tufts of grass arranged in certain ways; natural or manmade marks of almost any size and kind occurring almost anywhere that indicate a trail; and, to the detriment of the entire concept, the name of Glenn Beck and friends' misinformation blog.

---

[20] 'Passed by here the Adelantado Don Juan de Oñate, from the discovery of the Sea of the South, the 16th of April of 1605.'

Third, our world is full of things that look like blazes even though they are not. Rock and tree falls can knock out a chunk of tree bark identical to those made by humans. Animals (elk, porcupine) often eat the bark off of trees at just the right size and height and these marks can very much resemble a blaze.

To make things even more interesting, any of these can still be used as a blaze if the trail maker and trail follower so choose. And it gets more sketchy still; I was told by a Costa Rican farmer when I asked for directions that, "I needed to turn right, where the giant poplar tree used to be." It is a blaze, now only a memory, that marks the trail.

Which brings us to the fourth thing we need to know about blazes; they are temporary and depending on what they are made of, they can last from a few hours to hundreds of years — but in the end, they all will disappear. Forest fires or logging can destroy blazes placed on trees; weather will deteriorate paint, plastic and paper; visitors can and do destroy cairns, and natural erosion can take down even the most prominent of geo-formations.

Fifth, the definition of 'blaze' that we look for can be found in just about any dictionary. What is important about all 'blazes' meant to indicate a path toward something is that they do just that; they mark the beginning and/or middle and/or the end points of a path or trail — they signal that you are more or less where you are supposed to more or less be.

Recreation managers on public lands use eye-catching blazes and there are a lot of them. On the other hand, marijuana growers on public lands make their blazes hard to see and they are few.

Forrest Fenn, because of his interest in history and the out of doors, may well be attracted to the method used by the early trappers, explorers and settlers which was a hand-sized piece of bark cut out of a tree about eye level. But, especially for the game we now play, he would use a conspicuous natural landmark that would remain prominent for a long, long time.

However, as far as I know, Forrest Fenn is not in the habit of tagging anything or, for that matter, of knocking chunks out of trees with his axe; he probably used one that was already there — by which I mean the blaze, not the axe.

And last, about that title, *"Forrest Fenn to Star in Remake of Blazing Saddles."* I was kidding.

Are You In or Out?[21] My first reading of Forrest's *Memoir* was fascinating, the second was informative and the third left me with one monster question: "In the mountains somewhere north of Santa Fe?" I kept repeating it to myself. What bothered me wasn't whether his treasure was 'in the mountains somewhere NORTH of Santa Fe' or 'in the MOUNTAINS somewhere north of Santa Fe.'

My problem was with 'IN THE mountains somewhere north of Santa Fe.' The question that plagues even now is "How do we know if we are 'in the mountains' in the first place?"

Notwithstanding the absolutism of Senator Rand Paul and friends, there are things in this world that are relative and 'mountains' seems to be one of them. It's like when I showed a colleague from Brazil the Santa Fe River at maximum flow.

My colleague was a rather famous hydrologist who had taken his very first bath in the Amazon River and his expression on seeing our river was something like, "I've seen more water coming out of faucet leaks in most of the world's departments of water conservation. I brush my teeth with more water than this. What did you say it was again?" And thus it is with 'in the mountains.'

For example, if you find yourself standing in one of these 'crop circles' (center-pivot irrigation) just outside of Topeka and

---

[21] MtnWlk May/18/2013

someone asks if you are in the mountains, you would probably say, "No" (Figure 3).

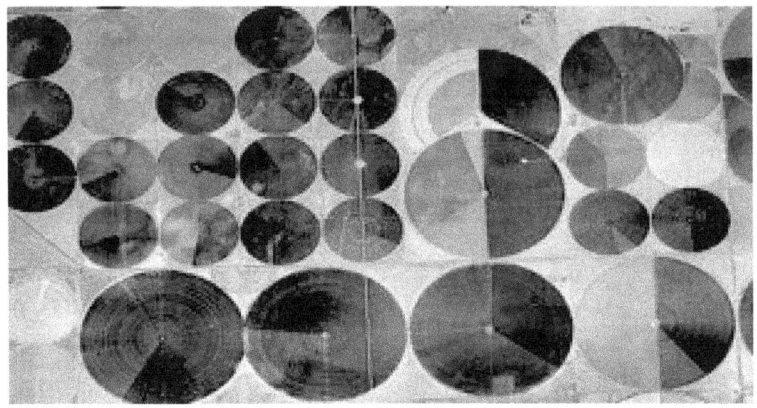

Figure 3: Center pivot irrigation near Topeka, Kansas. (Screen grab, Google Earth)

After all, these things only show up on relatively level ground and Kansas is, shall we say, 'relatively level.' What's more, nearby ranges like the Appalachian Mountains are a thousand miles to the East, the Rocky Mountains a thousand or so miles to the West, the Black Hills a couple hundred miles to the North Northwest and the nearest mountains to the South are several towering land-fills around Dallas.

Once again you are standing in a crop circle (Figure 4). But here the circles are 7000 feet above sea level in the San Luis Valley of Colorado and the nearest really big hills are the San Juan Mountains to the West, the Sangre de Cristo Mountains to the East, the Chuska Mountains to the Southwest, the Taos Mountains to the Southeast and a whole bunch of mountains to the North. Most of these mountain ranges are between ten and a hundred miles from where you would be standing. Now are you 'in the mountains?'

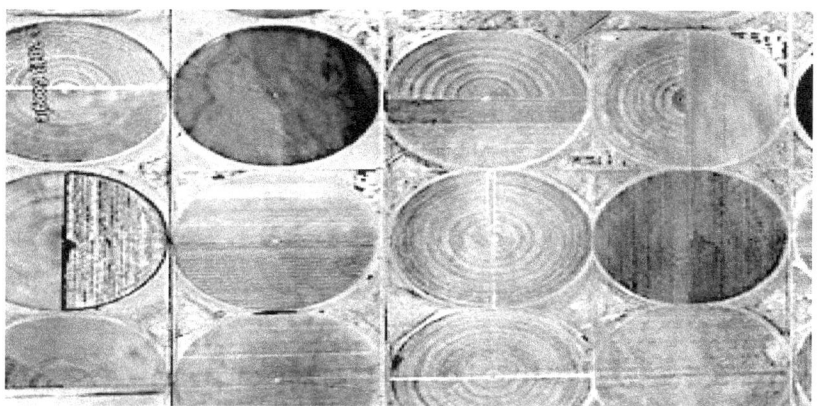

Figure 4: Center-pivot irrigation, San Luis Valley, Colorado. (Screen grab, Google Earth)

Here is one that may help (Map 1). As you can tell, it is a map of the Rocky Mountains and, since Forrest has given us the clue that the treasure was hidden in the Rocky Mountains, we know that the cache was somewhere in all that black. You must be careful though. Maps at this scale are terribly difficult to interpret at any detail. That doesn't mean that they are useless. For example, That slice of white between the bottom two black legs is the Española Valley, that is, the course of the Rio Grande as far north as Pilar or *Embudo* (which means 'funnel' in Spanish).

The leg on the left is a problem for me in that it extends too far south. So I sought out something that would explain it and found this (Wikitravel, n.d.):

> While the Jemez Mountains may look like part of the Rocky Mountains, they are distinct from the Rockies geologically, and are the remnant of a 'super-volcano' that had a catastrophic eruption about a million years ago, with several lesser but still significant eruptions since then.

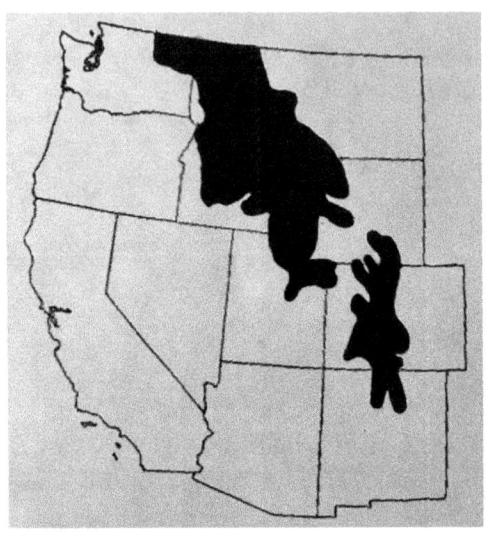

Map 1: Rocky Mountains in the Lower 48

The 'leg' on the left represents the San Juan Mountains which come south from Colorado and slim down to almost nothing a bit north and east of the Chama River.

With these exceptions, as far as I know, the dark area represents the 'Rocky Mountains.' So, in the lower 48 you are standing 'in the mountains' if you are standing anywhere represented by that black area. Hard to take, I know because what is also interesting about this map, apart from that 'mountain' thing, is that Forrest wants us to find a chest a bit larger than the shredded wheat box that sits on our breakfast table somewhere in all that black!

"This proves it. Sleuthy-Guy wants to lead us astray again," you say and you would be right. But I will leave you with this from my old buddies at the United Nations Environment Programme (Blyth, et al., 2002). Here is what they say about 'mountainous environments' which is the same as saying that you are 'in the mountains' if you are at an:

- Elevation of at least 8,200 feet; or an
- Elevation of at least 4,900 feet with a slope greater than two degrees; or an
- Elevation of at least 3,300 feet with a slope greater than five degrees; or an
- Elevation of at least 980 feet with a 980 feet elevation range within 4.3 miles.

I thought that was a fine piece of sleuthing until it occurred to me that it doesn't matter when *we* think *we* are 'in the mountains.' What matters is when Forrest thinks *he* is 'in the mountains.'

I'll work on that one some more because I doubt that Forrest has ever voluntarily read anything by the United Nations Environmental Program.

"You had a Good Home but You Left":[22] Here is a question we will have to answer to find Forrest's treasure. How far is 'Not far, but too far to walk?' Is it five miles? Ten? Twenty? A hundred? Doesn't it depend on how fast and how long one walks?

I mean, Meriwether Lewis of Lewis and Clark fame essentially walked from St. Louis up the Missouri River, over the Continental Divide, and down the Columbia River to the Pacific Coast — a distance of a bit over 3,500 miles. Lewis wanted to do that so he could make scientific collections of the plants and smaller animals that he would encounter (De Voto, 1955).

Likewise, many of the early Spanish colonists and friars in New Mexico walked from Mexico City to about thirty miles north of Santa Fe but they did so only as fast as the slowest animal they had with them — the speed and endurance of a pig that had to eat as it walked along (Simmons, 1988).

---

[22] MtnWlk Sep/12/2013

After Osbourne Russell and a couple of his trapper friends lost a fight (and their possessions) with the Blackfoot Indians, they made their escape by walking over the Teton Mountains at a pace of about 25 miles a day. Russell himself had an arrow through his thigh, none of them had eaten or slept much since the battle, it snowed during the walk and they made the trip without blankets and without much clothing. They kept this pace because they wanted to keep their hair (Haines, 1955).

On the other end of things, I am good for maybe two or three miles a day if the pace is slow and I get a nap after breakfast and lunch. But my pace is not the pace that Forrest is talking about.

We need upper and lower limits placed on the 'distance' part of the Poet's clues and to do this, we need to know how much time we have been allotted and at what speed to walk to solve Forrest's clue on how far 'canyon down' we need to go once we have figured out just where the 'warm waters halt.' Are there any clues to help us out on this one?

I can think of only one: Forrest was a military man and he learned a military cadence.

All of you know what a military cadence is — every military movie ever made opens with one. What is interesting about 'cadence' though, is that, as far as I know, there is no 'official' military cadence even though it is one of the more important parts of military training. Obviously, a cadence is meant to keep a tight formation and the lazy from lagging; but it also improves morale, promotes *esprit de corps*, and it reduces and postpones fatigue.

During formal reviews and during the Revolutionary War, cadence is/was kept by a drum. During everyday marching now-a-days, it is kept by a 'call/response' rhythm adapted from the songs slaves sang as they worked the fields and from the early churches.

There are probably hundreds of cadence 'songs' but most of them can't be given here because they tend to be a bit on the profane side of anything from the early churches. The title of this post is the 'call' part of a cadence that may no longer be used because of how tame it is: "You had a good home, but you *left*" as your left foot hits the ground. Then the 'response' is, "You're *right*" as your right foot hits the ground.

And so it goes. A military cadence is generally, but not always, about 125 steps of 30 inches each per minute for 'quick time' and 175 steps of 36 inches for 'double time.' Double time amounts to a mile every 10-11 minutes (Military.com, n.d.).

Even without unions in the military, during training, you get a ten-minute break every fifty minutes. So, one possibility for solving the distance problem is this: If we say that the time frame is one day then we can say the following:

- An eight-hour day with seven ten-minute breaks equals six hours and fifty minutes (410 minutes) of a cadence.
- At a pace of one mile each ten minutes, the distance would be 41 miles. This would be a jogging (double time) pace kept up for six hours and 50 minutes with 10-minute breaks allotted every now and then just so you can stiffen up.
- At a pace of one mile each fifteen minutes, the distance would be 27 miles.
- At a pace of one mile each twenty minutes, the distance would be a bit over 20 miles. This is the distance 'normal' people can generally walk in an eight-hour day given good conditions and good conditioning.
- At a pace of one mile each twenty-five minutes, the distance would be almost 16.5 miles.

So, for a one eight-hour day of walking minus a ten-minute break each hour, rounding things off a bit, and throwing in an unknown fudge-factor (like two eight-hour days), the place to 'put in below the Home of Brown' would be between 15 and 50 miles downstream from 'where warm waters halt.' That narrows things down a good deal and it is another 'cookie' for those of you in need of a cookie.

Tea with Olga:[23] The chapter 'Tea with Olga' in Forrest's *Memoir* has been responsible for any number of fruitless Taos Mountains snipe hunts by those who search for his hidden treasure. Those who hiked those mountains did so because they had read his *Memoir* and knew that he had cast the ashes of his neighbor and friend, Olga, over the Taos Mountains and that fact is thought to be a major clue as to where we were to search.

Maybe so, but I confess that I didn't go there. What I did do was spend a whole lot of time trying to decipher another bit of that chapter; something that I just knew had to be a major clue. It had nothing to do with Olga and the Taos Mountains; it was all about the tea.

I understand, of course, that even now, Forrest's IQ sits far above his age but what about his memory? I'm not much younger than he was when he wrote that chapter and I can't remember anything without my wife beside me to give me hints.

So how could Forrest remember, maybe years after the events, that Olga gave him red tea on one visit, and black tea on another visit, and then, after he had finished his task, that she would soon be drinking green tea with her father? And why was it important that the colors be mentioned anyway?

It all made me think that Forrest made things up for this part of the story. I mean, who ever heard of somebody from Texas drinking tea anyway? Texans drink 'blackstrap' coffee or boiling

---

[23] MtnWlk Jul/4/2012

hot cactus juice with the thorns still in it. There was something about 'red,' 'black' and 'green' that I really wanted to know.

So I did what I always do when something 'thinky' bothers me. I sat in front of my computer, counted the icons on my desktop, checked my e-mail, trashed a half dozen of the ones from the lottery supervisor in London, and dreamed about what I could do with the $28,000,000 I would get if I helped the widow of some deposed Nigerian despot.

And then, I thought of Google. I put in 'red,' 'black' and 'green' and immediately got back 482,000,000 results. I began to wade through them thinking that this was probably going to take all night when, on number 58, a Pendleton site showed that said the company had a series of national park blankets and that the one for Yellowstone followed the traditional color scheme for the classic quilts of its early hotels: 'red, black and green!'

I went through more of the results though I should have stopped at 58 because somewhere in the 70's, there was another Pendleton site that now had the Yellowstone blanket with the added color yellow and they were on a beige background. I doubted that the English or anyone else would voluntarily drink 'yellow' tea and this caused me to rethink my idea that the clue indicated only Yellowstone as the place to be; especially since the new Pendleton Glacier National Park colors were red, black, green and yellow on a white background and the one for Yosemite National Park had red, black and green on a blue background.

Feeling somewhat dejected, I began to page through *Teepee Smoke,* the beautifully done biography of Joseph Henry Sharp by none other than Forrest Fenn (Fenn, 1998). The book is illustrated with nearly 300 color plates of Sharp's paintings and a number of old photographs taken by Sharp himself.

I went through it once for the photos, and then again for the text, and once more for the paintings. And there it was; Sharp's near overwhelming use of the colors red, black, and green: vibrant portraits and scenes of everyday life of the Crow Indians and their neighbors the Blackfeet, Sioux, Cheyenne and Gros Ventre, painted while he lived among them.

Interestingly, all of these are tribes of the northern plains and mountains of Wyoming and Montana. Their territories were the Big Horn Mountains just east of Yellowstone and the foothills and valleys of the Absaroka, Beartooth, Gallatin, Madison and Gros Ventre ranges to the north, west and south of Yellowstone.

Sharp spent eight years living on the Crow reservation and often returned there after he and his ailing wife moved south. He, like Forrest, loved that part of the world. Its history and landscapes shaped their lives and, importantly, their work. Also like Forrest, for J. H. Sharp, 'south' meant New Mexico (Santa Fe for Forrest and Taos for Sharp) where he spent years painting the Pueblo Indians of Northern New Mexico.

So, once again we are nowhere but I still believe that the three teas of Olga make a clue the significance of which revolves around the colors of red, black and green.

The correct interpretation is still out there and I refuse to believe that Forrest wrote of the colors in 'Tea with Olga' only because he was preoccupied with a kitchen rewiring project and that he was just wanted to remember which of the wires (red, black or green) was the one he shouldn't touch.

What is the Value of a Fenn?[24] I'm sure the question has been asked before especially if 'value' means something more than dollars. For example, I can hear it being asked by Forrest's father-

---

[24] MtnWlk Oct/21/2012

in-law sometime before the wedding day and maybe by the Air Force Rescue Team as it went into enemy territory to pull him out after his jet went down over Laos.

However, I asked the question a long time before I even knew Forrest Fenn. No, that's not right. What I asked was, "Who uses what a Fenn has to offer" and who wants to change that use to something else?" But then the economists got hold of the idea and they are still trying to figure out just how to figure out the value of a Fenn. Currently they are running about, their comb-overs on fire, mumbling something like this (Tschirhart, 2009):

$$NV = \sum_{t=1}^{T=50} (PQ - C_f)(1+r)^t - C_p$$

What this says, if you are all that interested, is that the net present value (NV) of a Fenn is equal to the sum of all that other stuff with a discount rate of fifty years — clearly an error because the Fenn I know has lasted a whole lot longer than fifty years and I expect he's good for a few more.

Confused? I am. If there is any one group, other than attorneys, that absolutely confound me, it is the economists.

So, we need to go back to Forrest Fenn, especially since doing so may well give us one of the best non-poetic, non-age clues we will ever get. We can find it in his library.

Of course, I had never seen Forrest Fenn's library when I first wrote this but I suspect that somewhere in between his two favorite books, *Catcher in the Rye* and *Flywater,* is stashed a well-thumbed dictionary of some kind. I'm thinking that Forrest Fenn loved words more than he let on. He says he doesn't use them if he needs to look them up but that doesn't mean he doesn't know *each and every* definition of the words he uses.

'Forrest' and 'Fenn' are two of these words. After all, who among us has not sought the meaning of our own name? Mine is French for a worker in a salt mine — which would be appropriate except that I've never had a job that I didn't really enjoy.

Now, the first thing we need to know about these two words is where they came from because the double 'rr' and the double 'nn' are kind of weird. But, if you pronounce the double 'rr' and the double 'nn' just like they are written and roll those 'rs' in 'Forrest' and then when you get to the first 'n' in Fenn say it again while your tongue is still between your teeth so that what you get is 'Forrrrest Fennn.' Before you know it, you are more or less fluent in 'Old English,' which is good because that is where these words came from.

However, to get a definition of 'Forrest' is not that easy. Sure, you can drop one of the 'r's to make it Young English and find that a 'forest' is

1: 'A bunch of trees all bunched up' and
2: 'Woods' or 'wood'.

But the problem scientists have with these definitions is that all forests are not created equal — something far too complicated for laymen to look at here.

Suffice it to say that calculating a forest's value was a far easier thing to do when it belonged to the Shires or to the Romneys.

What about a Fenn? The 'definition' of a Fenn from an Old Englishman gives us a hint:

The aer nebulous, grosse, and full of harres; the water putred and muddy – yea, full of loathsome vermene; the earth spaing, vafast, and boggie; the fire noysome, turfe and lassocks – such are the inconveniences of the drownings"[25]

The Old Englishman who gave us this definition was obviously a developer who wanted to drain the Fenns of England and put in a series of subdivisions that, for marketing purposes, would have been called *"The Fenns of England One," The Fenns of England Two"* and *"The Fenns of England Three"* each offering *"Modyrn singele faemly hoomes starrting a ae mere foerty poonds six."*

But here is the real skinny. Fenns, or 'fens' as they are known today, are wetlands. Specifically they are periodically flooded marshy areas between a body of water and a forest. They may contain species of short woody vegetation like willows but mostly the high water table and flooding mean grasses, sedges, rushes, decaying muck, a sand lens or two and tadpoles. I have no idea if there is a treasure in there or not.

Sleuthy-Guy Finds a Mountain:[26] As we know from an earlier post, Forrest Fenn's neighbor and friend, Olga, called for him one day and an agreement was made (Fenn, 2011):

> When I arrived, her attorney was present. The mood turned somber when she said she was dying of cancer and needed a favor. Her plan was for me to spread her ashes on top of Taos Mountain and in exchange, she would state in her will that I could have her little rooms at their appraised value. She loved the sacred old mountain with its strong

---

[25] *A Discorouse concerning the Drayning of Fennes',* London, 1629 which I got from a fascinating blog called dawnpiper.wordpress.com/land-words. Accessed Oct. 20, 2012. Try it.
[26] MtnWlk May/9/2013

ponderosa and aspen groves that blanketed its landscape so completely. She said her father's ashes were there and she wanted to be with him again. The deal was soon struck, so we sipped black tea and nibbled on Oreos.

John Nichols was having a bad day: the roof had leaked again, the culvert that allowed him to cross the *acequia* to get to his small house was clogged and making a mud-hole of his driveway, the cesspool was overloaded and his neighbor's cows had broken through the fence, urinated on his old VW bus and smushed his veggies. This is what he then did (Nichols and Davis, 1979):

> I went to the back field and performed a ritual that often calms me down. From the center of that small patch of brome, I stared at Taos Mountain. It always soothes me, that mountain. It is the most personal geological formation I have ever experienced. I feel closer to it than to any mountain I have ever climbed, from Monadnock in New Hampshire to Pyramid Peak in the high western sierras. I'm not even sure I know the real name for the mountain...

Carl Jung, on a trip to New Mexico in 1924 paid a visit to Taos Pueblo and was ruminating on what it means to be 'in a place,' especially one like the one he was in.

> I stood by the river and looked up at the mountains, which rise almost another six thousand feet above the plateau. I was just thinking that this was the roof of the American continent... Suddenly a deep voice, vibrant with suppressed emotion, spoke from behind me into my left ear: "Do you not think that all life comes from the mountains?" An elderly Indian had come up to me,

inaudible in his moccasins, and had asked me this heaven knows how far-reaching question. A glance at the river pouring down from the mountain showed me the outward image that had engendered this conclusion. Obviously all life came from the mountain for where there is water there is life (Office of the State Historian n.d.)

SFGuy — somewhat of a Newbie to *Mountain Walk*, in response to a comment from Michael Hendrickson, confessed:

I am from Santa Fe and am embarrassed to say I don't know which mountain is Taos Mountain. I thought it was Wheeler but I understand you cannot actually see Wheeler from Taos proper, it is hidden by the 'foothills' between Taos and Wheeler.[27] I have been web searching and one of the first pages that comes up is a Wikipedia article on Taos Mountain. It says Taos Mountain isn't any one peak but actually the group of mountains east of Taos (MtnWlk comments, 2013):

Now, I understand that Wikipedia is probably not the best place to get information on a great number of things, but this one I totally agree with. The Taos Mountains are a short outside rib of the Sangre de Cristo Mountains that stretch from north of the Colorado-New Mexico line to Tres Ritos. So I responded with:

'Taos Mountains' is how I know them. One of those peaks may be called 'Taos Mountain' by some people. If that is so, it's a secret that I am not in on.

---

[27] Actually, at one time, Wheeler Peak was called "Taos Peak" (Ungande, 1965).

And then, there appeared in the comments, this one from 'Babylon Slim.'

> Taos Mountain is the holy mountain that is part of Taos Pueblo and down which flows the Rio Pueblo, its source being Sacred Blue Lake. All is sacred because it is where they believe they came from. All of Taos Mountain is off limits to non-indians. They enforce this rigorously. No one even flies over it (unless it is on the back side) out of respect. I never even heard of anybody ever just flying over it until I read what ff wrote. Behind it is indeed Wheeler peak and kind of...Taos Ski Valley. The Taos (spanish for Tewa) indians are one of the only pueblo indian tribes that have never been forced off their land. Indeed they own most of the acreage all around Taos — where they let their ponies graze. Visit their website or better, visit them but don't expect them to be very forthcoming. Go when they celebrate 'Feast Days,' ask a bunch of questions, take pictures and one of the tricksters will throw your ass in the cool waters of the Rio Pueblo. Enough?

You will notice, of course, that Slim's comment has a number of errors like, for example, 'Taos is spanish for Tewa.' Not to be picky or anything, but 'Spanish' requires a big 'S' just like 'Indians' requires a big 'I' and the members of Taos Pueblo speak Tiwa not Tewa which is the language of Ohkay Owingeh where I went to school; and, that the word 'Taos' isn't Spanish for anything. Rather it is what those early Spanish guys heard when the Indians said the word *'Tua-tah'* in response to the question of those same Spanish fellas who asked on arrival, *"A'onde hemo' llega'o, cara'o?"* which is translated as 'In the village' (by which I mean *'tua-tah'* not *"A'onde hemo' llega'o?"*)

Why are You Here?

Nevertheless, since Babylon Slim had 'unm.edu' attached to his name, I figured that I had better pay attention and did what anybody who grew up in Northern New Mexico would do. I sent an e-mail to 'Taos Mountain Outfitters' which said;

OK, People. With a name like yours, you seem to be the ones who can answer my question: Just where is Taos Mountain? What I have found, from in-depth looks at any and all maps and descriptions I can find as well as hiking into that area on numerous occasions, is (1) the 'Taos Cone' on the boundary between CNF [Carson National Forest] and TPIR [Taos Pueblo Indian Reservation] but mostly in the CNF (just east of Wheeler Peak); and (2) 'Taos Peak' which in on the boundary between the CNF and the private lands around Eagle Nest (NE of Wheeler Peak). Beyond that, I have found numerous paintings and photographs with the title of 'Taos Mountain' but they are always of what I learned were the 'Taos Mountains' or at least the southern end of that range, or, they are of the peak generally viewed as the highest from Taos which has the real name of 'Pueblo Peak.' Then, of course, there are the casino, a fiesta, a hotel or two, a couple of spas etc. that have that name. Oh. And you.

I have found references by nobody I trust that said, 'Taos Mountain' waters feed into Blue Lake and that the mountain itself is sacred to the members of Taos Pueblo.

Now, the 'Taos Cone' is a sacred piece of real estate to Taos Pueblo as is 'Blue Lake' as you know. But I cannot see where any of the water falling on 'Taos Cone' makes it to Blue Lake and it probably doesn't even make it into Rio del Pueblo unless one or two of your ex-staff members filled there canteens at Eagle Nest, trespassed to Blue Lake and did what understandably should never be allowed at Blue Lake. Help me out here.

Best wishes (and thanks), r/

Then, lo and behold, the nice people at Taos Mountain Outfitters immediately answered my query (which makes me think that all of you new people from out of state should at least pay them a visit) with this:

Hi Richard,

Taos Mountain is actually 'Pueblo Peak' on any map of the area. This is located on private Taos Pueblo Indian Reservation land. No public access to this area. Taoseno's refer to Pueblo Peak as Taos Mountain.

Water from 'Taos Mtn' sheds into the Rio Pueblo. Blue Lake sheds into the Rio Pueblo also.

Taos Cone is located in the Wheeler Peak Wilderness. Taos Peak is located east of Wheeler Peak Wilderness. Water from the Taos Cone sheds into the East Fork of the Red River.

Pueblo Peak is a mountain summit in Taos County in the state of New Mexico). Pueblo Peak climbs to 12,290 feet (3,745.99 meters) above sea level. Pueblo Peak is located at latitude - longitude coordinates (also called lat - long coordinates or GPS coordinates) of N 36.49114 and W 105.483064.

Taos Cone & Taos Peak are two separate peaks totally different from Pueblo Peak.

Hope this answers your inquiry re: Taos Mountain.

Thank you, Kim

Of course, some people (like me) who have suffered years in the vast wastelands of watershed management, will quibble a bit with this response.

For example, my good friend Kim says that Taos Mountain is really Pueblo Peak and then says that Taos Mountain (sic) waters shed to Rio Pueblo when even I, with one good eye, can see that the water — where there is water — from Pueblo Peak sheds mostly to the Rio Lucero which meets the Rio Pueblo just above the small village of Ranchitos where you can find the home of John Nichols, by far my favorite writer about all things Northern New Mexico, and who, by his own admission, does not know the real name of the mountain that he and others, including me, Olga, Forrest, Carl Jung, all members of Taos Pueblo, SFGuy, Kim and Babylon Slim so dearly love.

Playfair:[28] 'Playfair' is not an admonition — except for maybe two or three of you. Rather it is the name of a renowned geologist who got renowned when he figured out how stream tributaries interact with the streams they are tributary to. He even made up a law about it:

> Every river appears to consist of a main trunk, fed from a variety of branches, each running in a valley proportioned to its size, and all of them together forming a system of valleys, communicating with one another, and having such a nice adjustment of their declivities that none of them join the principal valley either on a too high or too low a level; a circumstance which would be infinitely improbable if each of these valleys were not the work of the stream which flows in it.

---

[28] MtnWlk Apr/27/2014

Playfair's law is called the 'Law of Accordant Junctions' and despite the very authoritative sounding name, the law is misleading. We can let the error slide, however, first because Mr. Playfair made it up in 1802 when a good portion of the U. S. population still believed that the reason the hills and valleys they lived in got to be hills and valleys was because of the Biblical Flood and, second, because Mr. Playfair had not yet walked the Big Horns or the mountains of Yosemite where glaciers had done their thing.

But it was close enough and because of the other things he and a few of his colleagues were doing, a new science was developed called 'fluvial geomorphology' — the study of how water acts to form what we see around us (Kennedy, 1984). They also made up some really swell words like 'thalwig' (the line within a stream channel that connects the lowest points at all sites of the channel); 'avulsion,' (a rapid change in the course or position of a stream channel by erosion to bypass a meander and shorten channel length and increase channel gradient); 'saltation' (the process by which sediment, of sand size and coarser, bounces along the stream bed); and 'comminution' which is the "process of reducing a mass to small, fine particles by impact or abrasion" (Figure 5).

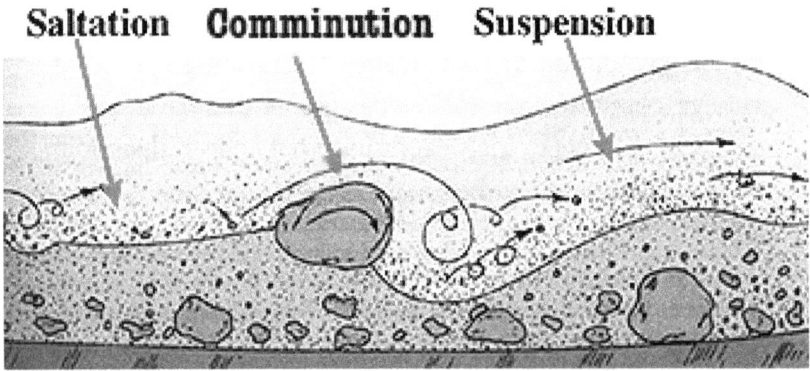

Figure 5: Actions that occur within streams (University of Maryland).

What does this have to do with Forrest Fenn?' Well, it's because when Forrest Fenn, the kid, waded the streams of the Rocky Mountains, he always ended up with sand between his toes and even if he wore tennis shoes, not only did he get sand between his toes, his shoes filled with pebbles. Forrest may or may not know what 'saltation' is but he certainly knows how uncomfortable it is to have the toes of one's tennies filled with rocks.

It also has to do with Forrest Fenn because river rocks have rounded corners for the same reasons –- all of that, 'saltation' acts as a never ending, incredibly efficient sand blaster that grinds away at anything that happens to be in a river including brass boxes and their contents.

Then, because there is a 'sedimentation' part that occurs wherever the 'saltation' part doesn't, things in a river disappear because they get covered in mud. And it all happens a lot more rapidly than we think.

The message of this treatise, of course, is that there is no way that Forrest Fenn put his treasure in a Rocky Mountain stream. Maybe you can still return your new waders and snorkel for a full price.

Boojums and Belly Plants:[29] As I think back on it, there were parts of my formal education that were noteworthy. I had professors who were the 'first in their field' or who had been students of the 'first in their field, which made me an academic 'son' or 'grandson' of some of the very best.

For example, I am the academic 'son' of Robert R. Humphrey, an ecologist who figured out the role of fire in natural ecosystems, and the 'grandson' of Fritz Warmont Went who, among other

---

[29] MtnWlk Feb/22/2013

things is famous for the Chelody-Went Model of plant growth — it has to do with hormones (Science Encyclopedia, n.d.).

Both of these men were characters. Dr. Humphrey, though deceased, is still the world's foremost authority on boojums and the nearest competition for that title is Charles Lutwidge Dodgson of snark hunting fame (look it up).

Dr. Humphrey made his living during the Great Depression by catching rattlesnakes in the Catalina Mountains and selling them to whomever happened to want a rattlesnake. Once, while on a family outing, he had caught two of them so his hands were full when he spotted another one. He made his wife take the first and his sister-in-law the second while he chased down the third.

Among many other things, Prof. Went was interested in the phototropic and gravitropic properties of monocot sprouts (look it up) and then he invented the climatron. Knowing this, if you fly over St. Louis and see that big round glass building at the Missouri Botanical Gardens you can impress your seat-mate by saying, "See that big round glass building? It's a climatron and it is there because of Fritz Warmont Went. And, when you spray your weeds with an herbicide, those weird, curly, deformed plant stems that show up are caused by Prof. Went's hormones."

When Prof. Went gave up his position in St. Louis, he went to Nevada and once again became a real botanist. He would take his students on field trips and after a while they would see him sprawled out on his stomach calling for them to come over.

Soon, they would all be sprawled out in a circle on their stomachs while he explained the wonders of the small desert plants in the center: "How is it that these tiny things can last through the drought and the heat and what does that mean for every thing else in this inhospitable place?" he would ask, just before he answered his own question. He called them 'belly plants' because only when on your stomach could you get close enough to really enjoy, as well as to learn from them.

These two professors taught me a lot of other things as well but what they taught me that is relevant to a treasure hunt is that both the 'strange' and the 'small' are very much worth a look.

Take Forrest's *Memoir* (Fenn, 2010). There are any number of things in there that are strange and some that are small and some that are both. The photograph on page 133 — the famous MAP page is a case in point. What you see there are a MAP, a coin, four gold nuggets and a Tirona gold frog with beautifully designed feet which are much different from the grotesque frog feet that Forrest put on his handcrafted bronze bell on page 134. Does this mean that Forrest believes the myths concerning the fearful denizens a fen supposedly holds and, thus, it would be a perfect place for his treasure?

Now, turn the page, and while you look at page 134, notice that the caption to the photograph says, "Ring the bell loudly—for he who dies with over fifty dollars is a failure." Then notice that 'dollars' in the caption is 'dollers' on the bell! That seems strange but then you read on the next page (135), the third and fourth lines from the bottom, that Forrest has given all of this ". . .a lot of thought because *little things* can be so important in our lives." Or is it that the spell check for wax figures is no better than that of Microsoft?

However, since Forrest grew up a latter-day mountain man, it may be that his spelling is no better than theirs — although it probably is better than mine.

We can check out that theory on pages 138 and 139, especially if we compare those pages to page 136. There, the caption to the photograph of an elegantly designed bell reads, *"Imagination is better than knowledge"* and the inscription on the bell reads, *"Imagination is better than knowledge."* It all looks good.

But then, in the text on page 138, he more or less repeats the words, in all caps, no less, and says, *"IMAGINATION IS MORE IMPORTANT THAN KNOWLEGE."* And, then, on page 139 he has placed two images of one jar with a similar inscription although we cannot see all of it; but what we can see is the word "knowledge" only here it is spelled "KNOWLEGE." Bad luck with the wax spell check again? Maybe.

However... when you look at the caption to those photos you see, *"Imagination is more important than knowlege"* even though a computer's spell check or the editor, or both, would certainly have caught the error. But they didn't.

So now I am confused. Why do the bells and the jars give the same idea but with different words and why is "knowledge" spelled correctly on one and not the other — including in the caption, the text and the jar?

I confess that I have no idea on this one. Please, can someone help me out here?

Brother Fenn Designs A Rainbow:[30] On maybe my 50th time through *The Thrill of the Chase*, I decided to list all the colors that Forrest mentions in the text because I thought that, just maybe, a clue would appear that could be the secret that would help interpret everything. Here is what I found:

The 'red,' 'black' and 'green' of "Tea with Olga," the 'yellow' and 'purple' flowers that grow just about everywhere in the Rocky Mountains, and the 'Brown' found in his clue-laden poem which everybody, including me, has taped to their bathroom mirror.

There is another 'red' as in Red Canyon, the site of one of his many misadventures. And then there is his first love, 'Bessie,' who was 'fawn' colored (which I'll call 'brown' to make things easier).

---

[30] MtnWlk Aug/1/2012

Then one could also include 'ruby,' 'silver,' 'turquoise,' 'emerald,' and 'gold' all of which are in his treasure chest, as well as the 'copper' clappers in the 'bronze' bells he forged instead of watching *Dancing with the Stars* like any normal American.

A couple of references to 'white,' one 'crimson,' another 'black,' a 'yellow' Cadillac and a 'brown' paper bag appear but all of these seemed material to the stories he tells and therefore probably meaningless as clues so I'll let them slide.

And then there is 'Ovaltine.' I don't actually know if this one is a real color but if 'chocolate' and 'coffee' are colors, why not 'Ovaltine?' I decided to skip it because I never liked the stuff anyway.

Forrest mentions 'Orange Crush' as being a heavy hitter in his bottle cap collection but, for reasons unknown, I have always been a Baltimore Orioles fan, and find it hard to include 'orange' in anything I think might be important.

The only 'blue' I found was in 'blue-gill' which has to be the all-time favorite catch of any young fisherman. They (by which I mean the blue-gill) will bite on anything including an eighth of an inch of worm left for two days drying on a #10 hook and they will fight you to the finish if you try to take it away from them.

When I finished with all of this, and after thinking about it a bit, I had eliminated every color except red, black, green, purple, yellow, and 'brown' which, taking them together, I called the 'Fenn Rainbow.' I asked myself if I had ever been any place in the Rocky Mountains where these six colors, in any way, were found fairly close together.

Then, while reviewing my entire life history with emphasis on ages 20-25 for no other reason than I suffer from short-term memory loss and have no idea where I've recently been like say, over the last fifty years, I decided that, 'yes', I had been in such a place and couldn't wait to consult with Google Earth to find it. I did and the coordinates for that place appear below.

Once again, I think I know the question you are asking, but the question I am asking is, "Is all of this information good enough to forsake August in Santa Fe with its sunny mornings, afternoon showers, mushroom hunting, mild temperatures, Indian Market and really, really great skies just to look for Forrest Fenn's treasure chest?"

Not really, so I decided that I would only do it if Forrest Fenn himself had ever had an interest in that part of the world. A short search showed that he did have such an interest since it is close to where the first and, maybe the richest, Fenn Cache was unearthed (Huckel and Kilby, 2014). The area covers about 150,000 acres that will require a good look. You can find what I found on any map of the Rocky Mountains at 41^0 13' 20.83" N and 109^0 47' 48.67" W.

Of course 150,000 acres sound like a lot but that's an area close to 50 miles long and five miles wide that can be reduced considerably if you find responses to the clues in his poem. Besides, 150,000 acres is a whole lot fewer than the 150,000,000 acres of another post which would amount pretty much to all the public lands in Colorado, Wyoming, Montana and New Mexico north of SantaFe.

So, I'll do it — especially since looking closely at beautiful places rich in history is why I signed up for this gig in the first place. Besides, my two and half year-old grandson wants to go along. It's going to be a great, great vacation.

See you at the end of the "Fenn Rainbow." All you have to do is figure out which end we're looking under.

CHAPTER 4

Where is it We're to go?

In Chapter 1, I said that one of the purposes of *Mountain Walk*, the blog, was to give my interpretation of any of Forrest's clues from his poem as well as any other 'clues' that I may find along the way to help you as well as to help me decipher the many languages he uses to confound us. Here are 10 posts in which I tried to do that.

Conversations with a Two-and-a-half Year Old:[31] I remember the first course in ecology I ever took and I remember it because it was mind blowing in any number of ways. It made me want to go to the library and find every book and article they had on the subject. I sat in the front row. I stayed after class and pestered the professor until either he tired or the next class wandered in. It made me see things and processes I had never seen before.

I wanted to know every little event that created any landscape that happened to be in front of me: its history of storms, fires and landslides, the burrowing and the bugs; who was winning and who was losing. I wanted to know about its washings and its dryings, what was permanent and what was passing, its temperature swings, who ate what or whom, and when and with what it all started. Ecology was challenging and oh so much fun.

---

[31] MtnWlk Jan/3/2013

Ecology is so much fun that I give an exam to all the Santa Fe visitors who are in good enough shape to walk the Rt 66-La Bajada-Camino Real circle with me. On the way back from that crazy incredible piece of Earth, I ask them to explain what they see as we break over the edge toward Santa Fe from the rutted Caja del Rio plateau.

It is a glorious scene with the southern extremis of the Rocky Mountains in the distance, the Santa Fe River course below, and a strange grouping of trees in the near view. It is that grouping of trees that is of interest because of how it is laid out — exactly like an orchard but the trees in it are not trees one sees in an orchard.

They are junipers — a small tree that is ubiquitous at this elevation and latitude and among its few uses are firewood for Forrest Fenn, subjects for artists to paint and a light wintertime snack for coyotes and scrub jays.

However, to plant junipers as an orchard would be a complete waste of time and money and contrary to common sense. It would be like planting goldenrod around a house in Maryland or Virginia. Out here, juniper is the plant that sheds pollen in the trillions and each little bitty pollenette with its mini-minute thistle-like spikes flies into your nose holes and then shuffles all the way up and through your sinuses. Within days of the bloom, which seemingly lasts from March through to October, the entire population of Santa Fe becomes a raspy-voiced chorus of crybabies.

But there that orchard is in front of you as if laid out by a band of teenage Future Farmers of America and if you can say just why it's there, you may have a leg up on trying to find Forrest's treasure. It means your powers of observation and logic are finely tuned and that your curiosity concerning things that just don't fit is close to that of my two-and-a-half-year-old grandson who has now entered the 'why' stage of his development.

Where is it We're to go?

This 'fine-tuniness' even helps if and when you read Forrest's *Memoir*. For example, you need to be aware that his picture captions come in two different fonts — one manufactured by a geeky engineer in Palo Alto and the other in Forrest's very own non-cursive hand writing. This became important a while back when my wife found a strange bit of graffiti on a rock, and when I compared the printing on the rock to the captions on pages 122 and 123 of the *Memoir;* they appeared to have been done by the same hand.

But, then, my wife announced that she wrote her alphabet the exact same way and proved it by showing me the New York Times crossword she was doing. Damn; so close and yet so far.

Sleuths don't let that kind of thing bother them. I went back to the *Memoir* and became aware that chapter titles come with chapter subtitles, and there, on page 126, I found a subtitle that said in really well hidden letters, "Somewhere north of Santa Fe."

Now we were getting somewhere. I leafed through the *Memoir* looking for more subtitles and found one that said, "Somewhere in Wyoming." "Aha!" I announced to no one in particular but my grandson immediately wanted to know what 'aha' meant and why I had said it.

I tried to ignore him. I was on to something. I took out my map of Wyoming and found that if you go canyon down the Shoshone River east from Yellowstone, you hit the Buffalo Bill Reservoir and, just below that, you have the metropolis of Cody, Wyoming (See pages 65-67, *Memoir*). Then I found that Forrest Fenn is not only a member in good standing of the 'Buffalo Bill Historical Center' in Cody, Wyoming, he is also a board member of that fine institution.

It was all coming together and I searched for more subtitles thinking that they would give me even more information. I found the clincher on page 58. It said, "Somewhere in Montana." My grandson shouted, "Aha!" but I knew that I had been defeated once again.

'X' Marks the Spots:[32] My grandson is now totally into the alphabet. I know this because the day after Christmas, the floor of our old adobe was covered with alphabetical blocks, alphabetical trains, alphabetical alphabets and alphabetical animals and he, like you, has now identified the Pirate's 'X' on Forrest Fenn's MAP as an 'X'.

Unlike you, however, he has not tried to figure out just where that 'X' on THE MAP is on the ground. I must say that it's placement was an enigma to me as well until my lovely wife, who is a hostess at the Book, Map and Photo Store of the New Mexico History Museum brought back a copy of a map that looks somewhat like THE MAP on page 133 of *The Thrill of the Chase* only it is much less fuzzy and a whole lot more colorful; all of which makes the 'X' become totally clear and its location instantly knowable.

Now, for those of you who are interested, the coordinates for that 'X' are 36°00'46.82"N and 105°31'49.40"W — except that they aren't. You see, I got those coordinates using a useless plug-in for Google Maps that must have been invented by a wannabe Google engineer working out of his mother's storm cellar in Temple, Texas.

If you want to know the real coordinates, you must use Google Earth, which now gives its own coordinates for any spot on the Globe. The spot we are looking for is at 36°00'39.98"N and 105°31'36.60"W which is not really an 'X' at all. Rather, it is the place where the invisible dividing line between Rio Arriba and Taos counties butts up against the invisible Mora County line for three arms of the 'X' with the fourth arm being an all too real

---

[32] MntWlk Jan/21/2021

ridge coming off of a 12,000 foot-high mountain in the Pecos Wilderness.

If, by any chance, you still want to go there, take the 'Divide Trail' (Forest Service Trail 36 via Forest Service Trail 27) which starts at the Santa Barbara campground and then takes you on a route that is kind of northy-southy over Jicarita Peak (12,835 feet elevation) and on to the ridge in question which would eventually lead you to a small peak of unknown elevation but whose name is 'Trouble'— at least that is what the map says. It would take the most storied star athlete from Taos, even one who is high on caffeine and riding a mule, a week just to get there. I am sure that it has been a while since our favorite mountain man and potential benefactor has made that trip.

However. If, once you are there, you take one or two very careful steps to the East, you can peek over the edge of a multi-hundred foot drop straight down to the easily reached 'North Fork Lake.' What if maybe the 'X' isn't exactly located at 36°00'39.98" N and 105°31'36.60" W but a few horizontal and a great many vertical feet to the East? Furthermore, you should know that this lake feeds the Rio de las Casas, a tributary of the Mora River which flows 'canyon down' right through one of my favorite places in all of New Mexico: Loma Parda!

You want more? My guess is that almost everybody in New Mexico, maybe even Forrest Fenn, knows that "Loma Parda" is Spanish for 'Brown Hill!' (Or, more accurately, 'brownish-grayish-dunish' colored). Not only that, one of the most famous hot springs in New Mexico is just a short jaunt south of Loma Parda at Montezuma!

Regrettably though, these observations are all backwards; the clues cited above need to go the other way. You *begin* with 'warm water,' then you *go down* the canyon, and then you *put in below the Home of Brown* — not the reverse. Not only that, but Loma

Parda is not even the '*Home of Brown.*' It is the home of a whole lot of snakes, a herd of passing buffalo from the Wind River Ranch, and Ben C. de Baca, the ghost town's only living human occupant.

No matter, Loma Parda is worth the trip. Ben, whose great grandfather and great, great uncle ran the 'Loma Parda Hotel and Taxi Service' back when the town was really jumping, is a man with a barrel of fabulously good stories. And he will tell them to you over a free soda-pop and maybe a *tamal* or two if he has recently been into town.

Turns out that Loma Parda's sole reason for existence was as the brothel for the soldiers at old Fort Union.

More Clues from Forrest Fenn Create Chaos Among the Faithful:[33] When Forrest is feeling really, really good — to where his playfulness outruns his restraint, he will give additional clues about the location of his hidden treasure. Over the past year or so, I have become privy to some of these extra bits of information because that's what we 'Sleuthy-Guys' do. I'll give you five of them — by which I mean clues, not Sleuthy-Guys.

1. "It's not in Nevada." This is a response Forrest gave to a woman when she requested that he come out to Nevada to collect the treasure for her because she couldn't manage it alone. It's a reasonable answer to a somewhat sneaky request but it's my belief that this is more than a well timed put down. It's a real clue and, who knows, he might continue to name places where the treasure isn't hidden and eventually things will get narrowed down to something manageable. For a long time my guess for the next area cut out of the running was 'Virginia.'

---

[33] MtnWlk Jun/19/2021

Where is it We're to go?

2. "Take a sandwich." When I first heard this clue I said to myself, "This is really going to be easy. You get up in the morning, have breakfast, go out looking, find the treasure, eat your sandwich and you are back by dinner." Not the case. 'Sir Conan' Dal almost always takes a sandwich and he is still out there looking (lummifilm.wordpress.com). Nevertheless, this one remains a good clue because of what it doesn't say. For example, it doesn't say, "Take a tent, a bedroll, a change of socks and food for eight days." It's a sandwich — just a sandwich although you might want to consider taking pepper-spray along if your sandwich resembles a freshly made Egg-McMuffin™ and you are taking it into bear country. Bears love Egg-McMuffins™.
3. "Take a flashlight." I don't have much to say about this one because, for me, any time a flashlight is involved things get scary. It's because I had a couple of aunts not much older than me who loved to scare the crap out of little kids and they did it with flashlights in dark cellars. In any case, this 'clue' could give new meaning to the very first line in Forrest's poem: *"As I have gone alone in there..."* Does that mean a cave? A tunnel? A haunted house? Or, it could be that '*...in there...*' isn't a clue at all and the treasure is hidden in a dark recess where a flashlight would be needed even if you didn't have to 'go into' anything. But then maybe he just wants us to see where we're going after dark even if we have no idea of where it is we're going.
4. "If you had its coordinates, you would be able to find the treasure." This 'extra' clue could be a game changer except ... well, you know. . . it's probably not. Still, like all of you who already knew of this clue, I immediately set off on a search of Forrest's entire *Memoir* for numbers (as well as to REI in search of a GPS).

And find them I did! REI must carry ninety different kinds of GPS', each one more complicated, and pricey, than the other. I immediately chose a yellow one, and then I went looking for numbers in his *Memoir* and found everything from the number 1 on up through 9 and then 0; and in any order and number of numbers you could imagine.

After a month or so of this, it occurred to me, sadly, that my new GPS may have been an impulse buy because this clue could have nothing at all to do with the hundreds of numbers found in Forrest's *Memoir*. As of now, my interpretation of this 'clue' is that it is a very polite swipe at the geocachers who go about the world hiding jellybeans, old hotel keys from Brazil and embarrassing photographs of their Ex in used plastic pill bottles for other people to find.

After all, Forrest was right; anybody can find anything if they have its coordinates *a*nd a GPS. Of course, and I am only guessing here, maybe it's his way of saying, "Geocaching is for sissies, and if you want to find *this* treasure, you will have to do it the old-fashioned way." Certainly I would never say such a thing myself because I really do love my new GPS.

Water Holes as Singles Bars:[34] 'It was a dark and rainy night' and I was wide-awake thinking about a problem in which I was to figure out one of those natural history things that can be oh, so frustrating, yet oh, so much fun: why did a shrubby live-oak chaparral species grow in profusion in some places and not in others just a foot or two away?

The next morning, I sat at my desk sucking on an acorn as I pondered the same question, when an ecology professor I knew stopped in and asked what was wrong. I explained the problem,

---

[34] MtnWlk Jul/19/2012

told him that I had tried everything and had come up with exactly nothing but a bag full of acorns. He stared at his corral dusted boots for a while and then asked if I had another acorn. I did. He popped it into his mouth and began staring at the ceiling to formulate his response.

Now, being a more or less observant itinerate, I have learned that teachers, mentors, and sages come in all kinds, shapes, sizes and ages and the cowboy who stood there beside my desk was about to become one of them.

He didn't say, "Try it this way," or "Try it that way," or "Try it all again." What he did say was, "Take a break." "Just go up there alone for a couple of days. Ride the back roads, look at stuff, and the only objective for the whole trip should be to have an ice cream cone in Sedona." (This was when Sedona had maybe five houses, a church and a rustic restaurant hanging out over the river that had the only freezer within 50 miles — I loved that place).

So, to quote Kit Carson and to shorten the story: "I done so."

And lo and behold, things clicked, eyes opened, the world smelled nice and ice cream never tasted better.

I tell this story because after spending more time than I should trying to fathom Forrest's memory as well as his tea drinking habits and finding that, 'red, green and black' led to a promising search area of more or less 15,000,000 acres north of Santa Fe, I remained stumped and thought of an old sage with dirty jeans and cowboy boots who sucked acorns. And then I began to secretly plan a trip to Yellowstone just to look at stuff; and, the sooner the better, because New Mexico was burning.[35]

Of course, this does not mean that preparation would not be required so I went once again to REI and bought their only book

---

[35] The Las Conchas Fire of June 2011, was New Mexico's second largest in history at 156,593 acres.

on the national parks of Wyoming and Montana and then ventured once again into the mind of Forrest Fenn via his *Memoir*. I finished the books in a couple of hours and began looking for more references on western national parks on the internet machine. What I found were a few hundred articles on geysers and waterfalls, several geology references and a bunch of articles on fishing.

Noting the quantity of space dedicated to fish and fishing in Forrest's *Memoir,* I then searched specifically, 'Fishing in Yellowstone' and got back a large package of interesting information like the fact that, although introduced into the waters of Yellowstone, the brown trout was one of the most sought after of the several species of fish that now occur there. Then I searched for 'brown trout Yellowstone' and got back — wait for it — a map of brown trout distribution in Yellowstone National Park.

Of course, brown trout have been introduced into nearly all of the coolish waters of the Western Hemisphere, including the Rio Grande, but that fact didn't slow me down. I went back to the *Memoir* and was stopped by the photograph of Forrest's 'Secret Fishing Hole' on page 124. What stopped me was that there was something vaguely familiar about it.

My mind went back nearly fifty years to a small lake in Puyehue National Park in Southern Chile. Rumor had it that this lake was full of brown trout put there by early 20th century German immigrants. I say, 'rumor' because friends and I had tried several times to catch said trout in said place and we were not only always skunked, we were also eaten alive by the fierce Chilean *tábano*, a horsefly the size of an actual horse that has a bite that will take large chunks out of exposed and unexposed parts alike. But then, one fall day after the first frost and the *tábanos* had all gone to wherever *tábanos* go for the winter, we walked along the stream that fed into the lake when I looked down and there it was — Forrest's secret fishing hole!

Of course, it wasn't really his secret fishing hole. His secret fishing hole is like 43°N, 110°W while this one was 46°S, 72°W — a difference of over 6000 miles. Nevertheless, the phenomena were the same; it was spawning time at the secret fishing hole.

I also noted the two pages of photos of Forrest's family holding the fruits of what must have been several days of really, really great fishing, with captions to identify where it all happened. Taking special note of the photo of a young Forrest standing in front of a water spigot captioned 'Water Hole,' I recognized the exact spot from earlier forays into web-world and made a memo to self to visit that spot and everything around it on my trip up north.

Forrest Fenn Renews His Poetic License:[36] When I reached the second grade at Lincoln School, I began to win all of the spelling bees. Indeed, Lincoln School hadn't seen anything like it before nor has it seen anything like it since.

But there was a problem and her name was Raylene Poe. I privately called her 'Rosy Poesy' and she sat two seats in front and across the aisle from me.

It didn't matter that I liked baseball and marbles and snowball fights and fishing like just about any other kid in class of my gender because mostly what I liked was recess and a good game of 'chase' where I could almost catch her. The thing was, she was a couple of inches taller than me and that was mostly legs. She could outrun anybody.

She also had long curls that cascaded to just below her shoulders and her breath was a pure mixture of grape cool-aid, Red Hots and flour paste. And, of course, the spelling part was just to impress her. In all the other classes what I did mostly was dream.

---

[36] MtnWlk Dec/11/2011

My favorite of my two favorite dreams was where Rosy Poesy and I were married and had two children and a bicycle and we lived next to a baseball field where I played for the Brooklyn Dodgers and hit nothing but home runs and laid down really, really successful bunts. In the other one I dreamed that she would come over to my house so that we could build highways together in the dirt under our big elm tree. We would use my favorite 'earth moving' equipment which consisted solely of a six inch piece off the end of a 2" x 4" and a potato. Of course, I would let her use the 2" x 4" because it made the best highways.

All this dreaming, however, meant that my arithmetic was horrible, my singing was worse, and my 'cursive' suffered so much that the teacher made me stay after school and make little 'o's and then big 'O's in long straight lines and she watched to see that my elbow never touched the desk. But I shined in spelling class.

Then, on the very last day of that very same class, I was sitting there just looking at the back of her head when she turned around in her seat, gave me her best second-grader Jezebel smile, lifted her foot towards me and there on the sole of her shoe was printed 'RP+RS'. I haven't been able to spell since.

My guess is that Forrest had a similar experience only it was in 'counting class' and if you want to know why I believe this, follow along as I highlight the nine clues in his now famous poem (Fenn, 2010, page 132) in which he tells us just what we have to do to find his treasure.

Where is it We're to go?

As I have gone alone <u>in there</u>
And with my treasures bold,
I can keep my secret where,
And hint of riches new and old.

<u>*Begin it where warm waters halt*</u>
And <u>take it in the canyon down,</u>
<u>Not far, but too far to walk.</u>
<u>Put in below the home of Brown.</u>

From there <u>it's no place for the meek,</u>
The <u>end is ever drawing nigh;</u>
There'll be <u>no paddle up your creek,</u>
Just <u>heavy loads</u> and <u>water high</u>.

If you've been wise and found <u>the blaze</u>,
<u>Look quickly down</u>, your quest to cease,
But tarry scant with marvel gaze,
Just take the chest and go in peace.

So why is it that I must go
And leave my trove for all to seek?
The answers I already know,
I've done it tired, and now I'm weak.

So hear me all and listen good,
Your effort will be worth <u>the cold</u>.
If you are brave and <u>in the wood</u>
I give you title to the gold.

So there it is; a poem with nine clues except that, if you have been paying attention, you already know that there are fifteen clues — not nine.

What, then, does this mean? Either Forrest had a similar experience as mine only in his 'counting class' and there really are fifteen clues or, he has pulled another Fensterism and we now must figure out just which of the fifteen are the real nine. Going on a treasure hunt with Forrest Fenn seems always to be interesting; but it will never be easy.

Note: After writing this, I put up a post which tried a 'wisdom of the crowd' strategy to see if all of us together could reach agreement on the nine clues. It was a complete failure.

So, I tried it all myself and used an adaptation of 'metes and bounds' mentioned earlier. For the metes (start at a given point, go a given direction for a given distance, then go a different direction and keep this up until you outlined the block of land in question and you are back at the start).

These are 'commands' and, to work, they should be followed in the order they are made. So I looked at the poem and listed the commands: 'Begin it,' 'Take it,' 'Put in,' 'Look quickly down,' 'Tarry scant,' 'Take the chest,' 'Go in peace,' 'Hear me all,' and 'Listen good.' What is noticeable from this exercise is that the first four deal with finding the treasure and the last five are what you are to do after the treasure is found. Consequently, I didn't use the last five as clues.

Then I looked at the bounds — those characteristics of the landscape that tell you when you are more or less in the right place: 'Too far to walk,' 'no place for the meek,' 'no paddle,' 'heavy loads' and 'water high,' and 'in the wood.' I used these five 'bounds' and the four 'meets' for our final solve. 'Found the blaze' is hooked to 'look quickly down' and the two are counted as one clue.

Forrest Fenn and the Curious Case of a "Poetic Hiccup":[37]
A friend of Forrest's, although not named here, is known for a great many things; but he will be remembered most widely for the following piece of inadvertent poetry:

> [T]here are known knowns;
> There are things we know we know.
>
> We also know there are known unknowns; We know there are some things we do not know.
>
> But there are also unknown unknowns—Things we do not know we do not know.

There is a fourth verse to this poem, perhaps purposefully left out by our accidental poet, or maybe it was skipped over because of a fortunate and timely hiccup or because of an unsuppressed full glottal stop — a high risk if one gives a press briefing soon after a D. C. power lunch.

The absent verse treats the subject of 'unknown knowns' which is a term with at least three definitions:

- That which we know but prefer not to admit;
- That which we know but it is suppressed deep into our psyche;
- Things that are known by a speaker or writer but that are unknown to the listener or reader in the context in which the listener or reader sits exposed.'[38]

---

[37] MtnWlk May/1/2012
[38] Morris, Errol. 2013. *Unknown Known.* Moxie Pictures. I wrote this blog post in May, 2012. Our definitions of 'Unknown Knowns' differ somewhat.

And so it is with the clues of Forrest Fenn. For example, he says that there are nine clues in his poem. I say there are fifteen — as reported in the last post (*Forest Fenn Renews His Poetic License)*.

That difference, a mere six of his counting fingers, was enough to bring an immediate response from Forest to the effect that, "Not only did the sheer beauty and ripening promise of Rosy Poesy create a vacancy on the spelling side of my brain, but I couldn't count to fifteen using all ten of my toes and the thumb normally stuffed up my nose" — or something to that effect. But that is nothing compared to what I am about to tell you.

Forest says that, in addition to the nine (fifteen) clues in his poem, there are, "A few other subtle clues scattered throughout the text" of his *Memoir (Fenn, 2010)*. After an intense, yearlong study of this *Memoir*, I conclude that not only are there more than a 'few' clues in there, some of them are not even subtle. As a matter of fact, I count a full seventy of them if you agree to the fifteen in his poem.

And that figure doesn't even include those non-clue 'clues' that caused some of you to fan out over the Taos Mountains, trespassing hither and yon, as if Forrest's clues were so simple that you just knew you would soon be dining on *pasta a la putanesca* at an outdoor restaurant in Milan courtesy of Forrest himself.

Now, a disclaimer or two: neither the term 'subtle' nor the term 'not so subtle' are the same as 'simple' or 'easy' and the idea of 'unknown knowns' does not necessarily indicate 'dissembling.' But when Forrest describes in detail the beauty of the places he knows, recounts their histories as if they were his own, says that he 'knew exactly where to hide the chest' and <u>then</u> lets us know that, "I even plotted to have my bones rest forever, in silent repose, beside the treasure chest," I begin to think that these clues are not subtle at all, and although they may be, for him, just descriptions of places that he loves and fantasies that he entertains, they are, by any definition, 'unknown knowns.'

He may not have meant them as clues at all but, for me at least, they are, indeed, clues of major interest. And, as such, they mean late nights at the Web machine searching out just where it is that, "… yellow and purple flowers flourish where no one is there to see."

They assure us of fascinating discussions to come with cohorts and family as we attempt to find the meaning of what he has written; and best of all, they mean yet another trip into the mountains.

"He Said What?"[39] It is over a year [now ten years] that I've been investigating the 'where' of the very spot Forrest hid his treasure. For months, Google Earth has been my nightly fare; all words in the POEM have been finely parsed and exegeted; I know which words are his and which he quoted and from whence they came.

I have chosen a potential site and analyzed the uploaded photographs on Google Earth of anybody who ever had a camera within a hundred miles of the place; I found the nearest post office, the library, the police station, the barbershop and the conservation non-profit; I know who their members are and what their mission is and I am now an e-mail friend of Chris, the only person there who evidently knows how to run a computer; I know where in the nearest town one can get a vegetarian pizza.

I looked for anybody named 'Fenn' or 'Simpson'[40] or 'Smith'[41] who ever lived in the county and found them all; I know who owns what piece of real estate over five acres in size within a hundred yards of both banks of the river; I am personally somewhat acquainted with the town's ailing, 90 year old unofficial historian and I have the local phone book nearly memorized. Believe it or not, I know Forrest Fenn's travel schedule for 2010.

---

[39] MtnWlk Jul/8/2013
[40] Forrest's maternal grandparents
[41] Forrest's 2nd or 3rd cousins.

I have located all points of legal river access anywhere close to 'the spot;' I know the stream classification according to USGS, USFS, USBLM and Trout Unlimited. I know its average temperature and flow rate at any given time between April 30 and November 1; I know the kinds of fish caught, their most sizable size and their spawning habits; I know the trespass rules and when the moose do their thing.

I have my bear spray ingeniously hooked to an air-horn so they go off together and, following Forrest's advice, I persuaded a friend to come along even though he knows that even with my new hiking boots I can surely outrun him.

I have eaten lots of raw garlic because only that can guarantee the mosquitoes will go elsewhere. My air mattress is once again patched. And, although I have yet to learn how to use it, the GPS has new batteries and I have a new really loud whistle.

The POEM? Piece of cake:

1. 'In there.' Check
2. 'Warm waters halt,' 'Canyon down,' etc. Check
3. 'Home of Brown.' Check
4. 'No place,' 'no paddle,' 'heavy loads' and 'water high.' Check
5. 'Found the blaze, etc.' Check
6. 'Why I must go and leave the damned thing.' Check
7. 'Tired and weak etc.' Check
8. 'Worth the cold.' Check
9. 'In the wood.' Check

Extra clues? Got 'em.

10. '300 miles west of Toledo.' Check
11. 'Not in Nevada.' Check

12. 'Not in a cemetery.' Check
15. 'No need to dig up outhouses.' Check
16. 'Over 5000 feet elevation.' Check
17. 'In the mountains more than 8.25 miles N of Santa Fe so stay out of his neighbor's yard.' Check
18. Colophon. Check
19. Fenn's Rainbow. Check

Other pertinent stuff?

20. Say "No" to guy in Santa Fe Plaza who tries to sell his interpretation of the clues for $3.50 each. Check

My team is ready. Mini-Sleuth has his little-bitty bottles, super big magnifying glass and teeny-tiny net to collect bugs and, unlike his father, he can identify poison ivy. We have made reservations in various motels and campsites and it is time to jump.

Then Forrest gives his latest clue. I call my team to give them the word: "Its not in Idaho or Utah" (Stump, 2013).

A Bone for You to Gnaw on:[42] Do any of you out there who were born after 1985 know what somebody like me does when they have writer's block? No, it is not 'clean the keyboard' or 'text your spouse' or 'hack the Pentagon.' It's things like 'walk the dog,' 'play with the cat,' 'search for a sharp pencil,' 'sharpen all the pencils you may have found,' 'raid the fridge,' 'get some coffee,' 'reread all the false starts,' and then give up and 'take a nap.'

I just finished a 'take a nap' stage but not because my muse has taken up residence elsewhere. It's because I have bluffed all the bluff I can muster and now I have to write something that will give

---

[42] MtnWlk Jul/24/2013

up too much ground and get too close to the secrets I have spent the last two years trying to hide. It is a costly thing, this thing I'm about to do and the rest of Team Sleuthy-Guy will be on my case ten minutes after I hit 'Publish.' It won't be pretty. Nevertheless, here it (the bone) is (Figure 6):

Have any of you ever seen a more blazey-blaze than this? "More blazey than what?" I hear you say.

"That white spot up there," I respond. "It has been there for years and will be there for many years more; and you have to look 'quickly down' because there isn't much more of an 'up' up there and, besides, if you look down from there for very long you get vertigo".

And it is big; about sixty feet by sixty feet and some 300 feet a.r.l. which is something only Forrest will know — the acronym, I mean. It is also canyon down and too far to walk from warm water and it is below a 'canyon down, home of Brown.' Not only that, it is a place that Forrest knows very well.

Figure 6: Blazy-blaze.

How do I know this, you ask. Well, if you really want to know and are paying attention, just across the river from the 'FEN' that is at the bottom of that steep 'FORESTed' slope, is one of those campgrounds where fisherfolk hang out and that serves really great breakfasts but they won't let you in if you are wearing waders and several years ago one of its patrons couldn't get the phone to work.

Now, it is my belief, based on an hour or two of super-sleuthing, that there is an excellent chance that, just maybe, that patron could have been none other than Forrest Fenn if, of course, it wasn't someone else.

You see, the mysterious patron had tried to place a call to Australia to discuss a buy he wanted to make of an item that had just been found and because the operator always gave him Shelby, Montana instead of Shelby, Australia, the largest gold nugget ever discovered anywhere now sits in some dinky casino in Las Vegas called the 'Golden Nugget' instead of in a brass box along with a bracelet of turquoise and silver that you are supposed to look for instead of reading stuff like this.

Of course, there are lots of collectors of gold, I know; but I dare say that only one of them likes really great breakfasts at campgrounds where fisherfolk hang out, that has bad phone service and who is also collector enough to want the very biggest of whatever he happens to collect at any given time — in this case 'gold.'

Besides, under the blaring lights of the Collected Works Book Store and the intense stare and unique line of questioning by Sleuthy-Guy, Forrest admitted that that very camp used to be a great place to find arrowheads.

Now you want a Cookie?[43] For the last post, I gave you what seemed to me to be the 'bone' that some of you had asked for. And

---

[43] MtnWlk Aug/6/2013

now I am being asked for a cookie? You know, don't you, that these 'gimmes' have to stop somewhere. But, here goes; you wanted a cookie, you get a cookie (Page numbers from Fenn, 2010).

We begin again with a photograph because of this fact: more photographs have been taken from the day Forrest Fenn hid his treasure till now than were taken in all the 150 years or so before he hid his treasure. Facebook uploads about 200 million photographs a day which makes about eight billion photographs a month and not one of them is mine. Even though most of those photographs are closeups of smiling crosseyed teenagers with their tongues out, that same technology should help you find your own cookie.

For example, look once more at the photograph I showed you in the last post (Figure 6). My wife and I had gone up north on a recon/intel mission because New Mexico was burning and old folks can't stand the smoke. We found this blaze and then found that Forrest knew the area very well. We saw that there was a 'fen' at the bottom of the cliff right next to the 'forest' that is also at the bottom of the cliff and so I took a lot of pictures.

Here is one that demands to be counted as a "cookie" since I have labeled a few of its more important parts (the blaze, the secret fishing hole, and the confluence of Cabin Creek and the Madison River (Figure 7).

Something that makes this cookie at least a gingersnap is that I talked to the fisherman down there in the right-hand corner. It was June and I had seen a couple of good sized rainbows just to the left of that big tree and when I told him about it, he said that a bit earlier in the spring, you could see hundreds of them in that spot because that is where they spawned.

I asked if 'browns' (Page 132) also spawned there and he said, "Yeah, they did" (Page 124). Then I asked him if he had ever been on the other side of the river and he said, "Yeah, he had crossed it earlier" and I asked, "How was it?" and he said — wait for it — "It's no place for the meek!" (Page 132).

I can hear the mistrust in your thoughts already but my wife could help me prove all of this except she had gone off downstream following an osprey to see where it was taking the fish it had just plucked out of the shallows (Page 121). Even so, we have now upgraded things to at least an 'Oreo' level.

As we parted, I asked the fisherman if he had caught some big ones and he said, "Yeah, but the best part of the whole trip was when he saw a moose come out of the forest with her calf" (Page 125).

Now, for sure, we have not just an 'Oreo,' but an 'Oreo with milk.'

But there is more. When we got back home, I studied all those photographs I took— especially this one (Figure 7).

Figure 7: Blazy-Blaze with Fisherman.

Notice the two trees that come together as a 'V'. You will also see that the 'V' is directly ('quickly') down from the white 'blaze' on the rock face (Figure 6).

If you look at these two trees a bit more closely (Figure 8), you can tell that neither of the blazes was made by a falling rock because they are on the down side of the slope and that they were not made by a tree fall because the tree that fell, fell outside the 'V.'

Figure 8: Tree V.

Now check out the point where the two arms of the 'V' come together, tucked away in that 'wooded' small cavity, you can see what looks like a metal pipe or even the end of a metal box (Figure 9).

That, my friends, is one of my wife's homemade chocolate-chip cookies if I ever tasted one and I have.

Figure 9: Could this be it?

A String of Pearls from Black Friday:[44] I'm out of cookies and out of bones, and because of my habitual tardiness, some of you now suggest that I am but a part-time blogger. That really hurts, you know? It doesn't seem to matter to you that my wife and I were doing some kickboxing a couple of weeks ago and she hit me with her left in-step on my right short ribs, and then I got a cold.

Of course only those of you who have ever had both a broken rib and a cold at the same time will understand, but let me tell you, such a thing is not all sniffles and hot tubs. It's COUGHING and

---

[44] MtnWlk Dec/2/2013

SNEEZING, and RETCHING and every WIGGLE sends little platoons of Texas militia guys with the quad-fifties they use to hunt cottontails shooting up and down the broken rib and then they zip across the break to have a go at the other side. My 'nursie' sister says its called 'healing.'

Just to show you that I do care about your puzzle-solving abilities even though the cookies are gone and the bones broken, let me give you what can only be described as a 'String of Pearls.'

First, lets say that a discovery has been made of a place on the side of hill that has a number of hot springs and the water from these hot springs heads downhill. ("Remarkable!" somebody snidely interjects. "Sleuthy-Guy knows that water runs downhill!" "Ha!" I say in response. "I know a place where the water runs uphill that my dad showed me 65 years ago and the place where it goes still isn't full!")

Now, said stream of warm water flows almost due south for a number of miles gathering steam until that rapidly growing stream of steamy water hits a much larger stream of cold water widely known for the number and size of its brown trout. You go down that cold water stream a distance that certainly fits within the 15-50 mile sashay that is 'not far but too far to walk' to a place that not only is full of brown trout but THE brown trout of record for that state once lived there, and a great many of his brothers and sisters still do.

You 'put in' below this 'Home of Brown' via totally legal access, and a short float of 25-30 yards brings you to an island in the middle of that river that is owned by neither the folk on the left bank nor the folk on the right bank nor by the USFS, NPS, BLM, SCS, nor any other of the feds including the United States Air Force Academy and the IRS. It is, however, managed by the State Department of Game and Fish, but they only seem to care if the willows are growing.

Further, this small island can also be legally reached by a couple of bridges over irrigation ditches and then a couple of short wades of ten yards or so across shallow, slow moving water. Even I could do it. Also interesting, is that this small football field size island is from 5002 to 5010 feet above sea level and is located at nearly the exact center (N/S and E/W) of what Google Earth calls the "Rocky Mountains."

And further still, depending on how one interprets it, "ΩΩ" could be the name of the small village nearest to the island, and it is all about 500 feet to the closest highway.

This is all true and enticing and the only thing wrong with the whole scenario is that this particular string of pearls didn't have a clasp and the pearls weren't tied off. So, they all rolled away and now you know how I feel.

Hope you all had a great Black Friday. I stayed in bed.

CHAPTER 5

When Things go South

Stuff happens: My dad worked around machinery all his life: winches, bulldozers, carryalls, whirring motors, conveyer belts, crushers, tractors, and superheated steam; and the danger of it all never caught up with him — until he retired. Then it was his electric lawnmower and three fingers.

The young know it all but they don't; the old know it all but forget. Caution is there until it isn't. Temptation can pull us along or it can push us over; it is always there. Those of you who are into sports know that even the best passing quarterbacks get intercepted and the best hitters in baseball get it wrong two out of every three times. Things do go south so what do you do when they do? I have no answers either but here are some thoughts.

Mr. Chini and the Tumacácori National Historical Park:[45] I dare say that those of you who don't like history don't like history because of all the names, titles and dates that come with it.

For example, Mr. Chini was born Eusebius Francis Chini in 1654 in Central Europe which at that time was called the Holy Roman Empire. And, as you will recall from your high school cheat sheet, it, by which I mean the Holy Roman Empire, consisted of many countries, cities, states, city states, counties, castles,

---

[45] MtnWlk Apr/10/2015

highlands, lowlands, clans and religions, all of whom passed the time by playing 'Game of War,' the object of which was to defeat your elder brother.

Of course, all of this gaming needed people in charge and people not in charge each of whom required a title and, therefore, we have, in no particular order, emperor, pope, priest, prince, prince elector, lord, knight, duke, minor and major counts, bishop, archbishop, abbot, prince abbot, elder, master, marques, friar, vassal, peasant, padre, bro, cuate, hermano and king, of which there were many. The ladies, of course, also had titles, one of which was 'lady,' but we will not go there. Suffice it to say that they also played 'Game of War' and though few had the 'moxies' of Kate Upton, they played it very well.

If you start counting from Christmas Day, year 800, as you should, the Holy Roman Empire lasted for just over 1000 years, until 1808 — a period which, obviously, makes for a whole lot of dates like, for example, 1492, 1517, 1521, 1540, 1540 and 1540 plus 1691, 1767, 1768 and 1821. You should remember those dates, and to help you do so I have prepared the following summary:

- 1492 Columbus who, as you know, discovers America by which we mean that he rediscovers the Caribbean a few thousand years after several small groups of curious Koreans walked over to the 'new' world just to see what was there.
- 1517 Friar Martin Luther places his 95 theses on the door of All Saints' Church to protest, 'the nepotism, simony, usury, pluralism, and sale of indulgences' by any of the Church hierarchy ranked above friar. Thus began the Protestant Reformation.
- 1521 This was the year the *conquistadores* finally destroyed the Aztec Empire for the richness of the Crown and glory

of the Church. Historians believe they were able to do this because the Spanish, by which I mean those who were from Greece, Morocco, France, Italy and Portugal plus a few Jews from Spain who thought it a far better gig than being burned at the stake, had been playing 'Game of War: Fire Age' while the Aztecs were still playing 'Game of War: Clash of Clans.'

- 1540 The year 4' 6" Ignatius de Loyola, being too short to play basketball at that university, organized the Society of Jesus (aka SJ, aka the Jesuits) to combat the Protestant Reformation by chasing down blaspheming Lutherans who kept breaking into subgroups just to confuse the Papists. The Jesuits were, by origin, the younger sons of wealthy landowners and as such, had no shot at inheriting land and title from their fathers as these were saved for the elder sons. Instead, the younger sons were trained at the best universities land and title could buy. Then, with nothing else to do, they became Jesuit priests. Meanwhile:
- 1540 John Calvin continued the Protestant Reformation by accusing the Lutherans of 'nepotism, simony, usury, pluralism, and sale of indulgences' and they, in turn, accused him of heresy.
- 1540 And, just to make history interesting, Antoine Saunier joins Antoine Froment in accusing the Calvinists of believing in baptism by sprinkle instead of baptism by dunk. The Calvinists accuse both Antoines of stealing from the poor box. Most of the Sauniers, however, remain loyal to the Pope.
- 1691 On what is probably his only visit to the place, Padre Eusebio Francisco Kino SJ (aka Mr. Chini) arrives in Tumacácori to establish one of his early missions. Padre Kino labored in the fields of northern Mexico and southern

Arizona for 20 years and established 24 missions, each with its farm and ranch enterprises and trade schools. When he died in Magdalena, Mexico in 1711, he became a future binational hero. The friars who had been sent to the mission at Tumacácori, however, were still trying to figure out how to fund a church building program when in . . .

- 1767 The King of Spain decides that the really smart, superbly organized, politically adept, and well resourced Jesuits were some kind of a threat. That is, they preferred to minister to the Indians than to the Spanish colonists which meant that their loyalties were to the Pope rather than to the King. He has them all arrested then force marched hundreds of miles to the sea for a long voyage back to Spain. The survivors are then 'cloistered' for the rest of their lives.
- However, the memory of the Jesuits lingers in the New World by which I mean the local folk still firmly believe that the Jesuits were very rich what with all those cows, farms, landed parents and dozens of plumbers and electricians from the trade schools paying union dues.
- 1768 Friars of the Franciscan Order take over the work of the Jesuits including the mission at Tumacácori and, in the spirit of true partisanship, begin to build a church that will outshine the dinky little edifice that the Jesuits had built. But, for lack of funding, it is all downhill from there for the Tumacácori Mission until . . .
- 1821 The successful Mexican Revolution: so successful that funding for the church building program at Tumacácori is renewed until Mexico evicts anyone not born there including a large number of the Franciscan missionaries. The church at Tumacácori is never finished — indeed, it seems to have gone backwards given a war with the United States, fights with the Apaches, an earthquake, floods, rain and other

acts of God. Additional damage is caused by thieves who tear off the roof for the timber and take out walls and the floor looking for Jesuit treasures of gold and jewels but find only the remains of two unfortunate Franciscan friars buried there long after the Jesuits had left by which I mean the Jesuits had nothing to do with building the building that supposedly held the non-existent Jesuit riches (Figure 10).

Figure 10: San José de Tumacácori

The moral of this story, of course, is that although you may not like it, you gotta think a bit about history before digging up all manner of sacred ground to find a treasure that was not buried there ever.

Permiso y Respeto:[46] I understand from my blogery colleagues that there have been some near misses of the close encounter kind

---

[46] MtnWlk Mar/23/2013

regarding trespass and just what belongs to whom — and it is all blamed on Forrest Fenn.

Now, I don't doubt that Forrest Fenn can be blamed for many things, but this one is best laid to our own DNA and to the space we grew up in.

The solution is simple according to my friend, Jose Villa,[47] who lived up by Alcalde. It has to do with *'permiso y respeto.'* I have a story to illustrate which involves a school bus. This bus is different in that it was short for its bulk and painted blue.

It sat at the back edge of a half-acre chunk of land carved from an even larger pile of mine tailings and the soil surface was black from the bits of coal that remained. A small kiosk and a pile of chairs, a '69 or '70 Grand Torino — the color of the soil — and a discarded sculpture made from Styrofoam and plaster which included a headless lady liberty and a base with painted dancing nymphs, also occupied the space. The whole setting was a bit surreal and begged to be photographed.

And it was. In a scene straight from a green-splat FBI movie, half a dozen cars screeched in from the highway and surrounded the blue bus on three sides as if it were a hideout for escaped inmates from the state penitentiary just up the road. A dozen or so 'agents' immediately exited the cars and surrounded the bus with weapons drawn: there were Canons of all shapes and sizes, EOS Rebels, Minoltas, Nikon D-40s, 80s and 200s; Powershots, and at least one Holga.

A late arrival, also filled with agents, skidded to a halt in front of the Torino and that was it; the fellow sitting in the Torino had

---

[47] Jose was one of Earth's beautiful people; a first generation immigrant from Mexico he picked cotton as a child. Then he picked up a PhD in Sociology and was a professor at San Diego State University for years. He was also an *Hermano* of the *Morada Alta* in Abiquiu, N. M. and a Chicano activist.

had enough and shouted to the last car that this was, "Private land, that the whole bunch of us were trespassing and that we should get out!"

Word that we were not welcome spread like wildfire through the agents still shooting into the fading light.

When I heard the news, I walked over from my position at the rear of the bus to apologize to the fellow now standing beside the Torino. After a while, he more or less accepted the apology and I stayed to chat. He said that the landowner let him live there in the bus in exchange for him guarding the kiosk and chairs which the owner would set up on weekends to sell things like soda pop and peanuts to the tourists which, more or less, was a custom in Madrid — the small village which we had just invaded. You have to understand Madrid if you are to understand this lesson.

Everything about the place is different from anything you have ever seen or heard, including how the name is pronounced — with a hard accent on the first syllable rather unlike that place in Spain with a similar name. Further, the break between syllables is also different: "Mád-rid" (New Mexico) as opposed to "Ma-dríd" (Spain).

Mád-rid is a wannabe art colony that has an ugly beauty about it favored by photography classes and workshops from Santa Fe. Piles of tailings are spread over the landscape and much of the town sits on this loosely packed spoil of the mining industry. Vegetation is scarce, buildings tilt and sink, and the water table is gone.

Years of abandonment or of temporary occupation by itinerates and souls with dreams larger than their pocketbooks, as well as a lack of trash pickup, have left mountains of decaying refuse that mingle with the even larger mountains of discarded and rusting equipment and decaying infrastructure from the mining days in the 1940s when Madrid was a thriving place full of young men and their lady friends.

Patriots all, they dug out thousands of tons of coal for the war effort and played baseball. The town boasted its own minor league team and a covered wooden stadium with real lights for nighttime games. To this day, its citizens remain patriots with parades and fireworks on July 4th, lights at Christmas, and, in this modern era, real trash pickup.

A few years ago, on a photo journey, I sat alone in that dying stadium and remembered a photograph from about 1930 of my uniformed father and uncles who were about to play a baseball game on a field much like the one I was sitting in but without the lights. I even imagined them playing there in front of me with their blousy pants, funky caps, and tiny gloves.

Of course there are other ghost towns like Madrid that have been converted into artist colonies in the last fifty years. Jerome, Arizona is one of these. But Madrid is different. For example, Madrid is set in the dry hills on the edge of the Galisteo Basin while Jerome is set in the dry hills above the Salt River.

The biggest difference, however, is that the hills around Jerome yielded up gold and silver while those around Madrid gave only coal. Thus, many of the buildings in Jerome were built of carved stone that today house millionaires while the buildings in Madrid were made of dry and cracking wood with asphalt shingles that blow off in the wind.

And while the wealth of Jerome remains gold and silver by way of artist studios, restaurants, and souvenir shops, the wealth of Madrid is in the curiosity, jealously guarded independence, and dreams of its people. They call themselves 'Madroids.'

The bearded Madroid who accepted my apology wore a soiled hat, a tattered shirt and blue jeans bought at a time when he had

had more to eat. Despite the beard, his wrinkled cheeks showed through and the color of his skin matched that of his boots.

He was particularly proud of his bus, which, he said, was given to him as payment for painting a house. He claimed that it had a 1961 engine in it that he had overhauled himself and that it would start right up if he needed it to.

I asked if he was from Madrid and he said that he was from Florida but that he had come to Madrid thirty years ago when it was still a real ghost town and although he had left a few times he had always returned because there was something about the place that drew him back. I said I understood and we agreed that everybody has some travel in them that needs to get out although it may take longer for some than for others.

He said he liked Madrid because of the dryness of air and the fact that the residents understood the value of what they had and that just about all of them had long ago discarded what was meaningless. He liked the grasses when they were the color of gold and he liked to explore the abandoned homesteads and to collect junk from the arroyos. I asked if he had any friends up in the cemetery and he said, "Yeah, there were some." He gave me the name of the owner of the land we were on.

As I left, we shook hands and I repeated my apology. He said, "No problem, Bro; just get permission next time. I'm sure you'll be welcome."

The Day I Learned Spanish:[48] We lived for nearly five years in South America during the first part of my career and I spent the rest of it wandering in and out of that fascinating part of the world.

---

[48] MtnWlk Nov/4/2013

During that time, my normal mode of operation was to arrange to meet with a few of the most knowledgeable folk wherever I found myself to let them tell me what it was like living where they lived.

One of those places was Pasto, Colombia — a sleepy little city high up in the *cordillera* just above the elevation where the coca plant grows best and where a few of the local wise guys had just tunneled their way into the bank — from the jail where they had recently been tossed. Pasto is that kind of place.

I stopped there on my way to Chile once. And to get things started on a project to have the local farmers convert their fantastically great cash crop to something like switch grass and sweet potatoes, I asked the fellow I was to work with if he could arrange such a meeting for when I got back in four days. Six or seven experts would be the right number for a good discussion.

Early on the day I returned, I asked if things were set and he said, "Yes, for 5:30." At 5:00 on the dot, we took a short drive to the university where we were met by its rector who looked exactly like a rector: dark suit, graying hair and mustache, and far too large a smile.

The three of us stood for about 10 minutes in a hallway of the school and then the door behind us opened and I was politely asked to go in first. I did and as I did, I heard a fellow on a stage, microphone in hand, announce to a 'small' group of about 200 members of the nation's Association of Geographers that the keynote speaker had arrived to give an hour-long address on 'Recent Advancements in Environmental Impact Evaluation.'

It was the first I new of it. As a matter of fact, it was the first I knew of the *Asociación de Geógrafos Colombianos*. Pasto is that kind of place.

So, I started off by saying that an hour was probably 55 minutes longer than the five minutes I hadn't prepared for and went on from there.

Mountain Walk versus Forrest Fenn

On the positive side, I haven't had a problem with public speaking in Spanish since, and that experience gives me the background to advise those of you who may attempt translation of Forrest's *Memoir* into Spanish — especially when you get to that part about the "Home of Brown" which, apparently, is where some of you are.

First, in his *Memoir*, Forrest admitted to a certain admiration for his Spanish teacher, but likewise said that he should have flunked the class. So a belief that Forrest Fenn could sneak in a clue in Spanish is probably an error. I've little doubt that the best Forrest could do is *"Houso da Browno"* and that his only other phrase of value is *"Dondi is la bano."*

The second error lies in translating 'brown' as *'moreno'* instead of what brown really means, which is *'marrón.'* Yes, I know that *'moreno'* can mean 'brown' but only in the sense of a suntan. It's like my wife commenting on how 'brown' my skin had become after I put the new roof on when what she really means is how 'dark' my aging skin had become.

Likewise, when a friend of mine admires the *'morena'* instead of the *'rubia'* when two of the 'girls from Ipanema' walk by, he is saying that he admires the one with dark hair over the blond no matter the skin color. On the other hand, when a young lady from Ipanema admires the *'moreno,'* nine times out of ten he is the one with dark skin. Thus, concentrating a search to the Moreno Valley of Northern New Mexico just because one believes it to be the 'Brown Valley' is flawed at best.

A third error has to do with the Cimarron River. That is, *'Cimarrón,'* though containing *'marrón,'* is not even close to 'brown' no matter how many of you walk that river in search of Forrest's treasure. The word means 'wild' as in 'runaway,' be it a plant, a horse, or a younger brother.

The fourth error — which is not so clear, has to do with the differences between *'casa,'* *'hogar,'* and *'querencia.'* *Casa*, of course means 'house' as in *"Voy a la casa"* which is "I go to the house." Generally, 'home' is translated as *'hogar;'* as the place where we sometimes eat, sleep and watch Seinfeld reruns. *'Querencia,'* on the other hand, is the term that best fits the 'home' in 'Home of Brown.'

At least that is how I interpret it and I do so because it best fits one of Forrest's 'unknown knowns' and it has to do with 'home' as a special place that carries a significance far beyond that building where we show up to eat or to sleep or to watch television or because it has free Wi-fi.

Conservation writers, landscape architects, and certain philosophers call the phenomenon 'Sense of Place' and for me, a very good articulation of the concept is given by Barry Lopez (1991) who uses the argument of *'La Querencia'* as the basis for his understanding of 'Sense of Place.'

That is, *La Querencia* is that spot in the bull ring where the bull goes to rest, to gather himself, to put aside the wounds from the lances, the darts, and the confusion that he has just been made to go through. It is that place where he gathers his strength and focus for the renewal of his fight with those who wish him ill. And he goes there because he understands it to be that very special place.

My guess is that such a place is the real 'Home of Brown' and Forrest knows it well.

The Carnoustie Effect:[49] Over the weekend, a friend loaned me his copy of the September 2015 *Outside* Magazine thinking that

---

[49] MtnWlk Sep/26/2015

Mountain Walk versus Forrest Fenn

I would be interested in the article, 'Cache X Money' by Peter Frick-Wright. I was.

The article is about an ex-cop living in Seattle named Darrell who made 17 trips from Seattle to Yellowstone and back over 17 months because he knew exactly where Forrest Fenn had cached his fortune. He was just going over to pick it up.

For those of you who want to compare, Darrell drove nearly 20,000 miles mostly at night and often through winter and spring snowstorms. In those 17 months he used most of his savings, nearly drowned trying to cross the Lamar River, spent the night freezing wet, and was picked up by Search and Rescue the next day.

Then on a subsequent trip he made it across the river but didn't make it back, spent another freezing wet night, and was once again picked up by Search and Rescue. This time, however, he went to jail for a few days and was fined $6000 to be paid in installments. Then, because he often showed up late for work after a weekend trip, he lost his job, got behind on his payments, and is now next to homeless.

Mr. Frick-Wright, who sometimes accompanied Darrell, mentions at least three times when Darrell 'lost it' after it turned out that the treasure was not where he was absolutely certain he had seen it either in a photograph or from a short but near impassable distance.

Despite all of this, Darrell remains a 'dreamer' and is still in the hunt for the treasure. "You want to believe that there's a treasure out there that's going to solve all your problems," says a loyal member of his support system.

Obviously Darrell's experience amounts to a whole lot of 'thrill' for a 'chase' that has left him with little but a few new acquaintances among the authorities in Yellowstone National Park. But, while an extreme case, he is not the only legend on the hunt for Forrest's treasure.

When Things go South

After nearly five years of writing this blog, I have come to know some of these legends and find them all (well, most) to be honest and unassuming people with interesting stories to tell. In many ways, they have taken on the personality of Forrest himself except that they tend to be more 'dreamer' than 'pragmatist.' And, without Forrest's pragmatism, dreamers will find zilch.

I, of course, have nothing against dreamers, dreams or dreaming. I personally have tubes of paint and empty canvases stashed away somewhere and every time my lovely wife and I stroll through the art galleries of Santa Fe, I say to myself, "I can do that,"— but I can't. For me, art was never an objective; it was only a dream.

There are major differences between the two, by which I mean (a) dreams and (b) dreams that come true.

Dreams just look out into a future or redo the past of make-believe while ensuring that your dream comes true requires any number of resources. Time, mobility, finances, a legal landscape in your favor and a plan come to mind if what you dream of is Forrest's treasure. And if you don't have the required resources, or worse, if you don't even know that you need them, you are, for want of a better word, 'screwed.'

"A plan?" you say. "Yes," say I, and it better be a good one. And I don't mean one that will just lead you to the treasure. I mean one that will also keep you out of trouble.

According to Forrest, thousands of individuals have looked for his treasure over the last few years, and, a good many of them have gotten into trouble while out there looking.

Preparation of a good plan is needed because the process of making a good plan castigates you when you're thinking is muddled, when it is founded on false assumptions and when your stated goals are mutually exclusive. It yanks you, dreamer that you are, back to reality. So, if, for some reason, planning gives you the hives or the hiccups so bad that you shy away from the word 'plan,' you are in for even worse suffering from what is known in the trade as the 'Carnoustie Effect.' Look it up.

Rappel, How to:[50]

> *"Rappel – to descend (as from a cliff) by sliding down a rope passed under one thigh, across the body, and over the opposite shoulder or through a special friction device."*
> *Merriam-Webster's Collegiate Dictionary.*

In the last post I presented the travails of Darrell as told by Peter Frick-Wright in the September 2015 issue of *Outside* where Darrell was absolutely certain that Forrest's treasure was in a small cave up the side of a cliff in Yellowstone National Park. Getting to that cave was a problem in that the easiest, if not the only, way was to rappel down from above.

After a few failed tries by Darrell and a friend, neither of whom knew anything of how to rappel except that it required a rope (which they had bought in a local hardware store).

These attempts were what occasioned one of the 'lost it' episodes mentioned by Mr. Frick-Wright (2015). He had followed Darrell through the snow and found him with his head against a rock and his new rope tangled in his snowshoes, crying.

On a far different scale is the 65' rappel made by Aaron Ralston in 2003 (Ralston, 2003). Mr. Ralston, you will remember, went alone into one of Utah's most famous slot canyons, scrambled over a 1000 pound chock stone which dislodged, rolled a bit, and pinned his hand to the canyon wall.

---

[50] MtnWlk Nov/17/2015

After a week or so trapped in which he lost 40 pounds, he decided that the only way to keep from dying in that lonely place was to amputate his own forearm, which he did with a dull knife and a twist of the arm to break the bones.

He then hiked down the canyon, which ended in a 65' rappel that he made, mind you, with a recently self-severed arm, more than a week of little sleep, nothing to eat, and nothing to drink except his own urine.

There are at least five things we learn from these stories:

1. Take a friend!
2. Tell a reasonably bright and attentive friend just where it is you are going and when you will get back.
3. Take a whistle, . . . and food, . . . and water, . . . and fire starter, . . . and some kind of shelter!
4. Do it wrong and you may have to drink your own urine.
5. Forrest Fenn didn't rappel for any reason; not to hide gold and jewelry, and certainly not so you could learn how to rappel. He prefers to jump from a cliff edge to the nearest tree and then climb down.[51]

---

[51] (Fenn. 2013) Forrest had shot a mountain lion from a 50-60 foot vertical cliff that was in between them. It was either leave the animal where it had died or a lengthly hike to get to the valley bottom. Forrest elected to jump to the nearest tree, climb down, collect the animal and walk out.

CHAPTER 6

Flotsam — No Charge

On Keeping Secrets:[52] I'm now getting to the place in this blog where I must be careful not to give away anything really, really important.

This has nothing to do with the caves on Jicarita Peak that I haven't yet told you about or the hot springs I have found over the years that sit just above and below the rim of that long black scar west of Taos known as the 'Rio Grande Box.' And it has nothing to do with the fact that my partner in this new pursuit may be worried that I will tell too much. I mean, he mostly likes to walk in the rain and jump into puddles.

My wife and I went to visit him early last fall and what we found when we got there was rain; It was the kind of rain that, if it occurred in Santa Fe, would find its way through every flat roof, skylight, and foundation in the county — even those featured in back issues of *Architectural Digest*. It had been raining for weeks, it continued to rain while we were there and it rained steadily until after we were gone.

In my long career as a more or less observant itinerant, I have discovered that rural folk, especially those in the southern hemisphere, don't worry about being out in the rain while urban folk, especially those in the northern hemisphere, spend a lot of

---

[52] MtnWlk Feb/5/2012

time trying to get away from it — the rain, I mean. The exceptions to this last rule seem always to be little kids and their grandfathers.

So, when things seemed to get a bit tense for those of us stuffed into a closed-up space, I would ask my young partner if he wanted to go for a walk in the rain. The response was an immediate break for the door; but only after we donned our raingear (T-shirts, shorts and sandals) were we allowed to go outside.

He loved the puddles; but a close second was when I would lift him up so that he could pull a crab apple off a tree and the pull would release a torrent of large drops that got into his eyes, nose and ears and make him squeal for more.

And then we saw the mushrooms: zillions of them in all colors and sizes. To be honest, I'm no mycologist but I do recognize a half dozen or so that are very good eating; and I know enough not to sample the others. I wondered if he knew anything about mycology.

Sure, the kid was only 16 months old but what the heck, it's never too soon to learn about mushrooms and neither his mother nor his grandmother were there to say, 'No,' so under my tutelage, before long he could easily tell the difference between a mushroom and a pinecone, between a mushroom and dog doo-doo, and between a mushroom and a Bud Lite can. I have no doubt that he could easily have mastered their scientific names as well except that, like the rest of us, he had trouble saying that weird Latin 'æ' sound.

All of this probably makes no sense unless you know that a friend and I had gone out earlier in the year to look for 'Brown.' We had set up camp and a very nice campground lady came by to make sure we hadn't placed the tent door over an ant hill and she told us that Game and Fish had recently shocked the stream and discovered several browns of 36 inches and pointed us in the right direction.

After about an hour hike up the trail that followed the stream, we sat down to rest and I took out my binoculars to see if I could spot an eagle, an elk or someone else looking for Forrest's treasure. Nothing.

What I did see though, was a fairly large pool at the end of a lengthy ripple in the stream about twenty yards below us. And in that pool was absolutely the largest trout I had ever seen outside of the Macho Pond at the fish hatchery just north of Pecos.

My friend immediately went down to count *coup* while I watched from above. To make a long story short, I will leave out the part where I took a nap while my friend did his best imitation of *nija* fishing, and say only that 36-inch trout do not get to be 36-inch trout because they are stupid.

On our way back we ran into a number of cows in a small meadow and while my friend busily practiced his dry-fly casting, I decided to take the world's most awesome photograph of a cow. It was when I zoomed out to include some of the landscape that I noticed the meadow was full of soccer balls.

Except they weren't. What they were, were *Calvatia gigantea*, the giant puffball; a royal member of the *Lycoperdacæ* family and a choice edible.

There were enough mushrooms in that meadow to have fed Napoleon's army with *soupe aux champignons* throughout his whole campaign.

Now you want to know where they are. No way. Mushroom finds are secrets more tightly held than are the solutions to any of Forrest Fenn's most difficult clues. You will have to find your own.

What do Tom Fitzpatrick, E. Jean Carroll, and Forrest Fenn have in Common?[53] This post is about getting lost and what you

---

[53] MtnWlk Mar/20/2012

need to get by until you find your way out. It is easier than you think; getting lost I mean.

For example, just last February an adult family of three was lost for six days in the forests of Oregon. They got that way while looking for mushrooms and for nearly a week they had little to drink and less to eat; they slept in a hollow tree and got frostbite.

And, again this February, a woman and her dog were lost for three weeks in Southern New Mexico. Just a few paces from the trail, they huddled together, drank from a stream and subsisted on a bag of pretzels. Getting lost is easy and it could happen to you — especially if you think you want to follow others who follow Forrest Fenn around a wilderness looking for his treasure. Or worse, it probably will happen to you if you think you are following Forrest but what you are really doing is following your own nose.

Tom Fitzpatrick, of course, is the iconic mountain man. One event that made him so happened in 1832 when, solo, he was ambushed by a group of unhappy Blackfoot Indians. He lost his horses and supplies in the fight and then lost his possibles sack, gun, clothes and knife while crossing a flooded river. For the next few weeks he took a circuitous route to his destination to avoid more Indians; he hid by day and walked by night eating nothing but buds and roots until found by friends out looking for him after he failed to show for the rendezvous at Pierre's Hole (Laycock, 1988).

E. Jean Carroll gave advice to the dateless, fashion-challenged, and dieters who read the glossy women's magazine *Elle*. Ms. Carroll is famous for once being selected as Miss Cheerleader USA; as a contributing editor at various magazines and for getting lost in the Star Mountains of New Guinea while hiking across that country with a couple of native warriors who wouldn't let her sleep in her tent. She rafted the Grand Canyon with a group of topless women and contributed to a book called, *Sand in my Bra*.

She once jumped off a 120-foot cliff into a flooded quarry and made her first jump from an airplane at age fifty. She lives alone on an island in upstate New York where she keeps a 'go-bag' — the modern equivalent of the mountain man's 'possibles sack.' She takes a back seat to no man.

Forrest Fenn, you have met. In his *Memoir,* he writes of the time he and his friend, Donnie Joe, got lost while camping in Red Canyon, Montana. The fish weren't biting, it rained a lot, and they could barely get a fire started. He also writes of a more important emergency when he had to bail from his crippled jet over Laos where he found himself in enemy territory, in a place he had never been, without his side arm, and with few rations and little water. Since he mentions neither a possibles sack nor a go-bag, we can assume that his storage container of choice was little more than his pockets.

Of course, the contents of a go-bag, a possibles sack and pockets depend on the owner's personality, their survival strategy and what they deem necessary in an emergency. Below is a table that compares what evidence suggests would be carried by Tom, E. Jean, and Forrest to sustain them through just about anything (Table 1).

Table 1: Possibles Sack v Go Bag v Pockets.

Tom Fitzpatrick POSSIBLES SACK	E. Jean Carroll GO-BAG	Forrest Fenn POCKETS
Leather for Making and Mending Moccasins	Meditations by Aurelius	Knife
	Photograph of Father	Pen/Flight Log
Tinder for Starting Fires		Three Baby Ruth Candy Bars
Flint & Fire-steel for Starting Fires	1 Bottle of Chartreuse	Matches

Extra Powder and Shot for Long Gun	5 Pounds of Mixed Nuts	Map for Starting Fires
	Ginger Snaps	Large Can of Black Pepper
	Block of Colby Cheese	Apple Juice
	Condoms	

The list for Tom reflects his life as a mountain man (Leacock, 1988). A knife, material for starting a fire, and extra powder and shot were what often kept these fellows alive. Their diet was simple and consisted of little but the dried meat of what they could kill. Leather was an absolute necessity because their moccasins wore through fast and often.

E. Jean's list is an emergency strategy of waiting it out. Indeed, she sometimes calls her 'go-bag' a 'no go-bag.' Condoms are included because, as she explains, "One needs to thank the men from FEMA when they get there." Had condoms been around during the early-1800s, the mountain men could have used a few in their possibles sack. Many tribes shared their women as a way to build alliances and this sharing was responsible for an epidemic of venereal disease among the mountain men which, incidentally, had nothing to do with a number of them becoming politicians later in life.

Forrest's list is an amalgam of some of what he had available during the two lost episodes he tells us about (Fenn, 2010). I have added his favorite beverage when he visits the Collected Works Bookstore in Santa Fe. His strategy to get out of these messes seemed to be something like, "What's a strategy?" since Lightening, his horse, got him out of the first one and his buddies in the U. S. Air Force got him out of the second.

What these three individuals have in common is not evident in the lists noted above because what they have in common is something intangible. I have no doubt that Tom Fitzpatrick would have made it to Pierre's Hole on his own; that E. Jean Carroll could have slept in her tent if she really wanted to and she could have made it back to civilization by herself. And Forrest Fenn could have walked out of Laos and back to safety without the help of anyone.

What they have in common is something else: it's pride, a near mystic energy, courage, stubbornness and self-confidence; things you and I may or may not have.

I recommend, therefore, that we not take off empty-handed just to see if we can make it in the woods. We'll be far more comfortable if we fill our daypack with water, trail-mix, space blankets, mirrors, fire starters, and, of course, some toilet paper. And don't forget your whistle.

Dream On:[54] For the new folk who have recently learned of the treasure that Forrest Fenn has hidden out there somewhere and are all charged up to begin the search, let me tell you what its been like for those of us who have been at it for a while. It starts off simple enough. You read Forrest's *Memoir* and pay some extra attention to the poem. You find a few addresses in the text thinking it's obvious that he put the treasure where he used to put other things. You make assumptions like, "It's hidden in the cemetery in Truchas, New Mexico" or "It's in the Red River just before its confluence with the Rio Grande." You begin a search of Wikipedia to find just where it is that gypsies hang out, or you try to make any and all numbers in his *Memoir* into geographic coordinates, and then you take out old maps from long ago trips to look for "Brown" as a street name, a park name, a town name, a county; but to no avail. And if you are really into it, you buy new maps but nothing has changed.

---

[54] MtnWlk Sep/29/2012

You go to REI and dream about all the stuff you will need to wade the freezing Fire Hole River and then you discover that the Fire Hole River is relatively warm. And then you say, "Aha!" and look at the map to find that the warm Fire Hole River meets the Gibbon River and you say, "Aha! The warm waters halt!" and then you discover that the Gibbon River also comes through a geyser basin.

You make plans to go 'out there,' 'up there,' or 'in there.' Your plans get more and more specific because your current theory seems to everybody but your spouse to be without fault. And then you find that where you wanted to go April 1 is still covered with 100 inches of snow.

All of us have been there. And because of these very high highs and excruciating lows I personally began to dream 'treasure dreams' but most of them were not the kind where I find anything. They were about the hundreds of caves scattered around the Yellowstone Caldera — virtually all of them filled with poison ethers and I try to figure out just how I could get in and out of the exact cave where the treasure is hidden in the 15 seconds I can hold my breath.

They were about the recent deaths of hikers in Yellowstone due to a bit of carelessness and hungry grizzlies that turned into nightmares about me looking for all the world like Hugh Glass, the mountain man who lost his scalp and half an ear and got several exposed and broken ribs in an encounter with a mommy grizzly (Myers, 1963).

Left for dead by his 'friends' he survived and, all alone, walked, limped and crawled through a few hundred miles of wilderness to a safe haven but, unlike Hugh, in my dream I roll into a river, float a ways down stream and end up in a pool full of piranhas.

The stress was getting to me. My adrenaline was flowing. I couldn't sleep but when I did sleep my dreams got even more intense and creative but all of them gradually fell by the wayside until but one remained to be replayed over and over. It did, however, include 'pay dirt' and it went like this:

> *As the virtual purple curtains open with the roaring MGM Lion looking exactly like a grizzly, a voice welcomes me in and invites me to sit back, relax and enjoy the show. But then, dressed in the tattered leather clothing of Lewis and Clark, I am shown wading the thunderous current of the Yellowstone River, its waters reaching to just above my nipples and its temperature reaching to just above freezing.*
>
> *Once across, I wave off an up-elevator full of people wearing three cornered hats and lapel pins that read, "Don't tread on me!" Instead, I climb the steep, rocky slope on my own. I find the treasure chest under two-feet of snow just minutes before the other guys (who now all appear to be wearing black spats and war paint) get there.*
>
> *The treasure is inside a small cave resting in an outer wooden box that I carefully open using the two omega-shaped handles that Forrest had thoughtfully added. I lift out the brass chest, dry a tear or two from my eyes, sniffle a couple of times, and wipe my nose on the pajama sleeve of Agent '99' who looks exactly like my sleeping wife. Then I replace the treasure with the still warm ham and cheese croissant sandwich that Forrest Fenn had insisted I carry along.*
>
> *"That'll show them who in this town has the real 'sleuthiness'" '99' whispers in my bad right ear, her lips just barely brushing against the long hairs that now grow from my earlobe and, as always, I don't hear a thing.*

Oh Six in Yellowstone:[55] I never met 'Oh Six' though she was a rather famous up-and-coming film star with thousands of admirers (Worrall, n.d). I thought that maybe I did see her once when we had gone out to look for Forrest's treasure and she and a companion were up for an early morning jog along the Lamar River but the whole thing went by so fast I really couldn't tell.

Oh Six' wasn't her real name, of course, but that is what her fans and the paparazzi called her. Her handlers, those who knew her real name and who followed her closely, knew of her travels, her fits of jealousy, her sexual affairs and her loyalty to those around her. But like all handlers of the famous, her's were also generally tight-lipped about such things as a way to give her some protection from both those who loved her as well as from those who hated her.

Hate is a strong word, I know, and I seldom use it to describe the feelings of anyone no matter how uninformed, bigoted, obtuse and downright frustrating they may be. But, as used here, the word is accurate. Those who hated her did so precisely because of her travels and talents, her habits and sexuality, her trajectory towards fame, her family and friends, and how, by force of personality, she dominated anything and everything around her.

She died in early December; killed by one of those whose hate was sufficiently intense to give no second thought to taking the life of another. I've seen nothing about just whose finger pulled the trigger and I don't want to know.

I wish that I could have warned her though; told her that where she was going was not safe. "No!" I would have shouted. "Don't do that!" "Don't go there!" But then, I didn't know her, had no way to make contact and it wouldn't have helped anyway.

---

[55] MtnWlk Dec/15/2012

I don't know if those who followed her every step, her handlers, tried to build a real protective capsule around her or not but my guess is that they didn't. For them,` it was a question of granting her a short, happy life of freedom or a longer unhappy life with freedoms restricted.

I want to think that I would have made that same choice for her but right now, I'm not sure.

Note:[56] I wrote *'Oh Six'* the night before the horrendous events in Newtown, Connecticut. The killing of Oh Six fades to almost nothing when placed beside what happened there. Indeed, I debated putting up the Oh Six post at all. In the end, as you can see, the post went up because there is, in my mind, a connection between the two.

I no longer hunt and don't now own a gun, but I am not against hunting — as long as there is a keen respect, indeed reverence, for the hunted. Anything less than that diminishes the hunter, the activity of hunting, and the culture within which the hunter resides. That is why the hate that killed Oh Six matters.

Likewise, I believe the Second Amendment to the Constitution to be an important part of that document though I disagree with interpretations made by the Supreme Court regarding challenges to that amendment. Like you, I have friends who believe the Constitution to be the final word; that the courts cannot place their 'modern' ideas above what the founders 'wrote down in plain English.'

Yet, they remain silent when I ask them why they hunt with semi-automatic, high powered, scoped rifles instead of a muzzleloader. Do these modern arms somehow raise the shooter's

---

[56] MtnWlk Dec/15/2012

skill level in the hunt? Accrue added value to a trophy? Or make the story more heroic and meaningful?

Neither do they respond when I ask them why they haven't joined the National Guard or the local police force if they want to play with weaponry that has no place in the sport of hunting or on the streets of any city or town in the United States. A 'well regulated militia' had meaning when the amendment was written and it has meaning now. But, neither then nor now does that have anything at all to do with 'concealed carry,' 'stand your ground,' or to private ownership of the implements of war. And I often wish that those who revere the Second Amendment would read the rest of our Constitution.

There is a debate that is needed in our country—a debate about freedom, and guns, and culture, and rules, and tradeoffs, and conflict, and fear, and pride and the moneyed interests that encourage something alien to citizen welfare.

But I fear that the debate is not going to happen; at least not in a meaningful way and the list of gun mayhem grows longer: Newtown, Connecticut; Portland, Oregon; Aurora, Colorado; Kansas City, Kansas; Manchester, Connecticut; Binghamton, New York; Blacksburg, Virginia; Littleton, Colorado; San Isidro, California; Hyattsville, Maryland; Austin, Texas and on most any street corner, alleyway, or parking lot in America on any given day.

Ezra Klein of *WonkBlog* who recently reviewed the statistics on gun violence involving multiple deaths summarizes the findings:

> Only with gun violence do we respond to repeated tragedies by saying that mourning is acceptable but discussing how to prevent more tragedies is not.

Sleuthy-Guy as Dance Judge:[57] Forrest lets us know that he has no affection for *Dancing with the Stars* although it took until page 139 of his *Memoir* to tell us about it. That, however, doesn't mean he doesn't dance. Doesn't mean he does either.

But I suspect that since he has always had that outgoing personality and given the photograph of the dapper young fellow on page 46 of that same *Memoir,* at least by Texas standards, what with the wide lapels and fresh haircut, at one time he knew the rudiments of dancing. Besides, he had a lovely Sweetheart and if the students at Temple High had any sense they surely named them their high school's 'Favorite Couple' and even with his being a Southern Baptist and all, there is little chance that he was a total wallflower.

Besides, the photo of that authoritative expression wearing a Temple letter sweater and white socks that sits on the fender of Bullet (Page 52 of *Too Far to Walk* — part two of his *Memoir*) kind of proves it.

And, what kind of a dancer was he? If I were forced to say, I'd say that he was more like a Sandhill Crane than a Broad-tailed Hummingbird and the differences are, ahh, large.

- The Broad-tailed weighs in at a little over a tenth of an ounce while the Sand-hill comes in over ten and a half pounds.
- The Broad-tailed has a wingspan of five and a quarter inches and an overall length of four inches whereas the Sandhill's wingspan is six feet plus and its length nearly four feet.

And the dancing is likewise, a mismatch.

- That of the Broad-tailed male is aimed at a specific object of his 'affection' who just sits there watching and measuring

---

[57] MtnWlk Nov/3/2014

it all, by which I mean there are a whole lot of horizontal figure eights over a space of a couple of feet and then a series of flights of sixty or seventy feet straight up and then straight down. Once he wins that pretty little thing, he is on to the next.
- Then the poor girl gets to build the nest herself — a labor of about a week at four hours a day in which over thirty trips an hour are made. The result is a nest of anything small and fluffy and enough spider-web to hold it all together. In the end it resembles an empty half of a walnut shell camouflaged with a bit of moss.
- On the other hand, the dance of the Sandhill is a lot of bowing and curtsying, and hopping by lifelong partners who seem to have gargled with several pints of Sprite each to keep their hydration up. And then all the neighbors join in the fun until the whole wetland resembles a full-blown rave at its height with most of the moves you would expect: head-banging, jumping, fist-pumping, shtomping — even twirking . . . a whole lot of twirking.

Sandhill nest building is likewise totally different from that of the Broad-tailed Hummingbird. Both parents are involved; it takes place far to the North and is the work of individual pairs.

On our very first mini-search for Forrest's treasure over ten years ago my wife and I stumbled on a nest-building duo just a few yards from where some believe Forrest's inadvertent clue in *Too Far to Walk* will lead them and that was a long time before he decided to mistakenly put that clue out there for all of us to see.

The Big-Birds stood together and every 20-30 seconds the male would bend down to pluck a stick or a leaf or a two-needled lodgepole pine fascicle from the water as the stick or leaf or fascicle floated by. He would then toss what he had found to his mate who would add it to the pile of other sticks and leaves and fascicles and then sit on them, wiggle a bit, stand up, adjust the pile some and try again. We watched until dark and though we weren't formally introduced, we named them 'Bubba' and 'Peggy.'

Philosophizing:[58] Active searches for Forrest's treasure chest seem to slow in late fall and stop altogether during winter — kind of the opposite of what the mountain men did. Beaver pelts reached their best quality during these periods and though the trappers had to hunker down during the heaviest snows and when temperatures in the mountains dropped to bone-chilling levels, the work of trapping went on.

When outside activity was impossible, they stayed in their crudely built huts or in their buffalo skin teepees, told lies to one another and 'philosophized' (Leacock, 1988). So, since winter is here and my sweet wife is now deep into remodeling our 17' long Casita (which we will take to Southern Arizona where we are volunteers at the Tumacácori National Historical Park), for the next couple of months, this blog will do the same (by which I mean I also will tell lies and philosophize). Here goes.

One of the topics that often comes up when people discuss the places they love is a concept called 'Sense of Place.' You may not call it that, but I've no doubt that you have felt it.

There are hundreds of writings out there that discuss the topic. Architects, land-use planners of various kinds, conservationists, deep ecologists, photographers and a sociologist or two, write most of them. Some of the writings are scholarly tomes, others are scientific studies and others are just downright beautiful

---

[58] MtnWlk Jan/8/2015

descriptions of a specific place that, if read alone late at night, bring moist eyes and throat lumps.

Still, though the musings on a sense of place are each different from the other, they do have some things in common. For example, I dare you to read any of them without stopping from time to time just to remold the concept and make it your own. Other similarities are that they describe places that demand either protection or attention; and, though the descriptions are deeply felt, they are often preceded or followed by a statement that the concept itself, is 'fuzzy.'

I had never really thought about that fuzziness thing until one day a friend and I were riding along in his old jeep station wagon with the observation deck on top somewhere between Rowe and Las Vegas, New Mexico. We were discussing a recent photography book that had a page or two on a sense of place and he asked me what I thought it meant.

Having never thought about it at any depth, and therefore I could opine, I offered the first thing that came to mind. "Banter," I said, "It has to do with banter."

Fortunately, we were fast approaching the corner where we were to make a very important turn lest we wind up in Trementina rather than Watrous and the conversation died.

That was a while ago and now that I have had time to think about it, I find the statement that, among other things, a sense of place has to do with 'banter,' to be perfectly justifiable. You see, a solution to the fuzziness problem can be helped along if, instead of emphasizing 'place,' as most writers do, you emphasize 'sense,' as most don't.

Emphasizing sense rather than place takes you to what you feel and understand about a place rather than to what you see and think you know. It has to do as much with what is inside of you as it does with what is out there in front of you.

If you can banter within that place, it says that you are comfortable there. You know enough about it to hold an intelligent conversation. You can make jokes with those with whom you trust and defend yourself when things get more serious. Likewise, you know enough of the culture and language to recognize the difference between a tease and an insult. But, in addition to its beauty, you know enough of the dangers of that place to be cautious but not afraid. And, you know where you are, even if you are lost.

I've no doubt that Forrest understands the concept very well; that is why he has a specific place that has meaning to him, a place where significant life passages were taken, where he conquered beasts within, where he learned a great deal because of the battles that were lost as well as won, where he smiled and laughed the smiles and laughs of freedom, and, because of all this, it is a place where he would like to be laid to rest. If we discover just where that site is, we have found the treasure. I'm convinced we will also have discovered one of the Earth's beautiful places. As far as I can tell, his aesthetic choices have always been impeccable.

Remembrance Day:[59] In our pre-teens, my brother and I would work on an uncle's farm in northeastern Colorado. The farm, though operated by an uncle — the brother of my father, was the farm of great uncle Soren — the brother of my paternal grandmother.

The property was part of what had been a much larger farm that suffered what so often happens to such acreages. They are divided among the heirs and then divided again and again and eventually sold when the resulting parcels become too small for anything that approaches a real living.

Great Uncle Soren was born in Denmark as was my grandmother and when they were just kids, the family immigrated to America

---

[59] MtnWlk May/25/2014

and crossed the country from New York to eastern Colorado in a covered wagon when buffalo still roamed the prairies.

I knew Uncle Soren as a curmudgeonly old fellow with an awkward gait who chewed tobacco, preferred Frank and Maud, his team of horses, for farm work over such things as tractors; bought a new pair of bib-overalls once a year, and seldom ever acknowledged the presence of us kids.

On Sundays he would ride Frank to the nearest small town for church and to collect his mail. He never married and lived alone in his part of the old farm house where he cooked his meals, collected feel-good stories from magazines like *Readers Digest* and played his favorite hymns on an ancient, squeaky violin before going to bed.

I know this — the collection of stories — because I came to be the owner of some of his belongings a half-dozen years ago and the stories were pasted in several old notebooks. Also among those memorabilia were yellowed and decaying newspaper clippings that told of his time as an elected county official, a photo of a young Soren, an article from 1914 saying that he had left for Europe having volunteered to fight in World War I and then a shorter, later statement, a notice really, that he had been seriously wounded.

It saddened me that I had known none of this before — that he was once young, that he was bright and involved and brave and full of tales that he would never tell and that now are lost forever.

When the treaty to end that war was signed at the eleventh hour of the eleventh day of the eleventh month of 1918, the United States set aside "Armistice Day" as an annual holiday now known as "Veteran's Day" and the awfulness of that war has been diluted to something that celebrates all of us who have served in the military with free access to national parks and museums and a whole lot of furniture sales.

Elsewhere though, in Europe and the British Commonwealth, it is called 'Remembrance Day' meant as a time to reflect on the horrors of war, the loss of loved ones and the assuredness of death. There is no celebration there.

But we do have 'Memorial Day;' a holiday that began as a time in the spring when flowers could be collected to decorate the graves of all those who died in our own Civil War. But this has also been changed and now we decorate the graves of all of our fallen from all of our wars and we wear t-shirts with flags on them, watch a flyover by the National Guard and discard the ads for more furniture sales.

And so, for my friends Guy and Jim and Forrest and Larry, for my cousins Kenny, Keith, and Don, for my uncles Roy, Everett, Rizz, Ron, Clearance and Wesley, for my Great Grandfather Constantine, for my Great, Great Grandfather Francis, and for my Great Uncle Soren, let me leave you with the wisdom of some of our greatest warriors:

Every gun that is made, every warship launched, every rocket fired signifies in the final sense, a theft from those who hunger and are not fed, those who are cold and are not clothed. The world in arms is not spending money alone. It is spending the sweat of its laborers, the genius of its scientists, the hopes of its children. – *Gen. Dwight D. Eisenhower*

Ours is a world of nuclear giants and ethical infants. We know more about war than we know about peace, more about killing than we know about living. We have grasped the mystery of the atom and rejected the Sermon on the Mount. – *Gen. Omar N. Bradley*

I have known war as few other men now living know it and nothing to me is more revolting. I have long advocated its complete abolition as its very destructiveness on both friend and foe has rendered it useless as a method of settling international disputes. – *Gen. Douglass MacArthur*

Our chiefs are killed…the little children are freezing to death. My people…have no blankets, no food…my heart is sick and sad…I will fight no more forever. – *Chief Joseph*

During that Great War to End all Wars some of the most horrendous battles were fought in Belgium at a place called Flanders Fields — now the home of row after row of the graves of those who died there. Twenty-five of them are inscribed with the name of Fenn.

It's All on Me:[60] It's all on me; by which I mean that I keep warning you all to stay vigilant, mind your manners, play by the rules, take a whistle, take water, take food, watch where you step, take a buddy, stay safe and what do I do? It's a long story.

A couple of retired University of New Mexico and state water experts and a photographer wanted to go see a place where water and water wars had really meant something. So we went to the Rio Puerco and Cabezon — a surreal place with volcanic plugs, salt-water rivers, artesian wells, limestone blocks, and ghost towns.

And then I broke my leg. Mind you I was just standing there by the side of the road when up jumped a whole block of fossils. When I first saw it, it was flat as flat can be and steady as any as it lay there on the ground. However, if I had had my walking stick, which I ALWAYS take with me and which I always insist that

---
[60] MtnWlk Nov/28/2015

everybody take as well, I would have tested the rock's stability to see if it was, which it wasn't, or to see if it more resembled a teeter-totter which it did.

When I stepped on that flat piece of limestone, it sent me rolling backwards down a 30%-40% slope as if I were a slinky. I would go head first, make a pile then feet first and make a pile. During one of those feet first stops my right foot decided it had tired of the game and stayed in a crack it had slipped into but the rest of me kept going. I heard a couple of 'pops' and wound up about 40 feet down the slope with my right foot facing several degrees from where it should have been facing.

Pete found a couple of blankets and a pillow in his car and threw them and some water down to Jim who was just getting to me. He then took off down the road in his car to find a phone signal, and Henry stayed up on the road in case anybody with any sense came by.

About 40 minutes later the HOTSHOT crew from Jemez Pueblo showed up and an EMT came down; stabilized my leg, and with ropes, sled, neck brace, belts, and grunts I was out of there in about an hour, most of which was a physical.

You hurt? Yes. Where? Lower right leg. Move your fingers? Yes. Move your toes? Yes. Pain in back? No. Need to throw up? No. Hit your head? No. Bleeding? No.

He called up for a neck brace and what looked like a sturdy sided shoebox, ripped enough of it away for my foot to fit inside and then called for another box to fit my entire leg into; he taped the boxes shut and put the neck brace on. He called for a companion and a light litter which they tucked under me; then called for a sled and a rope. They lifted me into the sled, belted me in, tied the rope to the front end and pulled me out.

The results? So far its one tibia, one fibula, three pins, two steel plates, 18 screws, 42 stitches and some real nice conversations with the nighttime nurses in the University of New Mexico Teaching Hospital. The doctors say it will be a long one, putting more and more weight on it as time passes and maybe a few hours a day with a cane by mid February.

There is something weird going on in nursing in that they can't be nurses anymore: no pats on the arm; no rub of the shoulder — has to do with lawyers and harassment.

But not for Rosa Cowboy, the strong boned, 50ish, Navajo nurse who gave me my nighttime feel good shots. A slight smile showed on her face when she noticed I was watching; when she finished, she patted the back of my hand — an acknowledgment that I was human, that she knew I hurt, that she was there if I needed her.

She closed the curtains, lowered the lights and left a small crack in the door as she went on to other duties. I love those people.

Gone:[61] Like all guys, those of us going through our early teenage years in Northern New Mexico were borderline perverts and certifiably stupid. We laughed in all the wrong places, threw rocks at one another, blew things up, had acne, and became experts at snapping wet towels at bare buttocks in communal showers. Worse, we thought that, *"yin-yang"* was the funniest word that anyone had ever invented.

And then we were forced to take a class called 'The History of World Civilizations' taught by a snarky immigrant from Ohio who, as he conned us into reading what became our very first real book, said that even *we* had a place in there somewhere.

It worked though. Mike whizzed through eight years of college in four years and became a scientist at Los Alamos. Bobby was a standout tackle at New Mexico Highlands on his way to becoming

---
[61] MtnWlk Sep/9/2014

a history teacher himself. And though raised with a whole bunch of siblings in a two-room adobe just off NM 285, Walter was voted most likely to succeed and became a respected politician.

Those friends are gone now, taken out in three separate automobile accidents along dark New Mexico roads. But we learned something in that class: that there were a great many other fascinating places that the Española Valley did not encompass, that things were a whole lot more complex than fishing the Rio Grande, that wars have been with us forever, and that *yin-yang* was much, much, more than a word for the human nether regions.

That ancient Chinese notion of interrelated opposites: of 'light and dark,' of 'hot' and 'cold,' of 'illness and health,' and, especially of 'home and away' fascinated us because it seemed that both the *yin* and the *yang* of 'place' were required if either 'home' or 'away' were to have any real meaning.

And that is why my lovely wife and I are once again homeless.

We've had a case of the 'goings' for a while but for many reasons it didn't happen and now, all of a sudden, we are gone. We've sold the house that we built and the home that we loved and traded it all for a small r. v. trailer decorated with wild flowers and filled with the aroma of well-brewed coffee. We've moved on to new adventures; to add new friends and to nurture our time with old ones.

Have we spurned Santa Fe? Sporadically. Santa Fe is a tough place to get rid of.

Do we still chase after treasure? Absolutely. 'Thrill' grows on you and there are lots of treasures out there.

Is this the end of *Mountain Walk?* Nah. Sending y'all down fruitless paths is way too much fun.

[But I never wrote again.]

CHAPTER 7

A Penny for Your Thoughts

When I started *Mountain Walk*, I soon figured out that a blog, to be a bona fide blog, needs a real comment section. Here is a selection of the comments received on *Mountain Walk*. I re-looked at all of them — the many good ones, the ones that made me laugh, the ones that made me cry, the poetic ones, the ones that created relationships that I hope will never die. I even read the ones from folks who appeared a bit chippy and from some who were lost in their own sadness and hate.

There were long ones and short ones and some that I wished were shorter than they were. I never locked anyone out as an individual though there were a couple of strings where I eventually did lock down the discussion. So, here are my selections.

The Short Ones: You will notice similarities within the group. They were made by Newbies, most of whom stayed around for quite awhile because once you are in with the 'thrill of the chase,' it's difficult to get out.

- I've narrowed it down to two possible locations, both of which fit very well, except for the darn 'blaze' part. . . — Clint, March 1, 2013
- Its in there, its in the wood. — Pete, March 9, 2013

- I have located the blaze. — Ron, March 16, 2013
- Its in a mine below the brown home at the abandoned brown mine ... — Jerry, January 16, 2016
- A possible location of the treasure is at Fox Lake, MT off the beaten path. It matches the poem. — Gold, Sept. 10, 2015
- I don't know but I feel that I might have a good idea as to the general location ... — Jeff, December 13, 2018

Now, I don't mean to poke fun of Pete, Ron, Jerry, Clint, Jeff, or Gold. They did their best for never having read Forrest's book. Many of us more or less did the same thing.

However, just to compare, other searchers for other things had resources far beyond anything we could imagine and they couldn't find what they looked for either. And, I don't in the least find it difficult to make fun of them.[62] Here is my choice for the stupidest hunt remark ever:

> We know where they are. They're in the area around Tikrit and Baghdad and east, west, south and north somewhat.
> — Donald H. Rumsfeld. March 30, 2003.

The Naysayers:

> The hunt is just like the lottery it makes poor people even poorer and the chance of you finding the treasure is about the same chance you might be struck by lightning in the forest fen!
> — Mark, May 2, 2013

---

[62] The United State Government has 16 intelligence agencies with about 100,000 employees. It has satellites, spies, listening devices and a gazillion dollars worth of software. They did not find evidence of WMDs in Iraq.

Mark, Mark, Mark. If the gambler is you, your comment is wrong in soooo many ways. How much research do you do before you have that lottery ticket in your hand? How far do you walk to get to your favorite convenience store? Do you ever take your family with you? Is it even a family affair? Do you teach the young ones about the wonders of nature on your way to the gas station? Do you ever see an elk or a bear or a bald eagle or a beaver dam while you wait in line to buy a ticket? Do you have a photographic record of the parking lot? Do you then share the heroic stories about which lottery number you chose? Rethink it my friend.

Some Favorites: One of my favorites of those who faithfully 'attended' the comment section was Sancho. Sancho had this idea that the whole chase was centered on Tierra Amarilla, N. M. and El Vado Lake (As did a number of other searchers that included some of the more mercenary of our colleagues).

If I had to describe Sancho (even though I never met him nor talked to him except for our sparse conversations in the comment section), I would say that his entire life, save for a stint in the military, was set within 100 miles of Chama, New Mexico. He would be between fifty and seventy years old and his ancestors would have arrived in Northern New Mexico nearly 400 years ago.

He would be a loyal member of the Brotherhood, the Hermandad, the group known to outsiders as Penetentes, whose morada would be located in a place like the villages of Canjelon or Cebolla. He would be polite but suspicious of anybody named 'Saunier.' He would have a property of 5-10 acres with an apple orchard and alfalfa as the understory. Best of all he may also have a family heirloom chile handed down through 8-10 generations.

Sancho liked to test me to see if I was really from Northern New Mexico. The phrases in bold in his note below are examples. For those of you who read Spanish, it probably looks like we have our own language and, I guess, we do. Apart from a few *alebados* that I didn't look at in any detail, I don't think I have ever seen more than two words of written Northern New Mexico Spanish.

Quando la ayates? Yo le feguro Que ase mas que un ano. Y si no staras serca o te canstes de buscar. De todos modos este ano algen lo va ayar. Yo se que sabes endonde sta. Tambien yo pero es en onte sta peron. Bien yeno de cuevas y vivodas. Y la berea quasi ya ni se. Y las cuevas stan tapadas con piedra mas pesadas que la fregada. Y las pesadas stan muy lejos pa caminar solo y los mansanas se elaran otra ves. Ajina es pa esos rumba. Si no la ayastes y me quiers audar deja me saver. Y si nos pega la suerte la jayamos lo apartenos todo por la metada. **Tamvien si me entiendes y pedes leyer esta nota, le fegero que meres norteno,** *y si nor eres y no me qiers audar tira lo en el bote porqe aiy es pa donde te qiero llevar y ensensar la piedra esha de lumvre. Y si te busta ir a la trucha trite to vara aotigo si qiers. Sta serca de, los indios, pero no es privado. Som deja me saver. No sta scrito vien pero esta scrito para que lo entienda uno que nasio qerio. O como diease e tio qaido. Dejame save.*

Con mucho respecto. sancho

So I answered him. But if you aced your high school Spanish class (maybe especially if you aced your high school Spanish class) don't worry if you can't read what is written here. You learned that Spanish is a precise language. What we have here is not a precise language. This is written according to what one hears — first and final consonants are often eaten or swallowed whole, schwas show up in the strangest of places, 'b' replaces 'v' and vice versa, words are combined, and the letter 'r' somehow becomes the letter 'd'.

Celebrate it. Its a language hidden for 500 years and spoken by folks who didn't even realize it was a language. It just was. I hope I get to meet Sancho someday.

> *Que uvo Sancho? Onde as etao? Save que yo no la he ayao. Ni ceda. Leo ben la nota. E como leed albo scrito ace años peo asi havlan os denorte. Me da gana' ved as cuebas peo no me da tempo agora. Julio o agosto? As viboas molesta peo las septo com parte de la natudalesa. Stoy sigudo que el Sr. Fenn no camino enderos tapaos asi que stoy eguro que el no ha echo esa caminata. Dame el numero de telefano pa fija nafecha bisitad as cuebas.*
>
> Saludos, r/

So, What is a Learning Curve? And then there is this string of comments initiated by 'ERM.' I like to think of it as an example of Forrest's chapter on, "Jump Starting the Learning Curve" (Fenn, 2010).

> [Y]ou've seriously missed the point SAUNIER, with your weird thoughts of microsoft and spell check and whatever else you've mumbo jumboed about…geezus i can't even believe you went on about his spelling??? these images are ARTIFACTS, which means they're probably old, and in case you didn't know the english language has evolved for a very long time from other languages, and whoever handcrafted these items had they're own way of spelling them, and, in his captions he merely wrote what was engraved on them, then in his own print he "corrected"

them according to our modern spelling....go to colledge (lol). — ERM. February 28, 2013.

My response:

Hi ERM. May I ask if you have a real name? The 'artifacts' were crafted by ff some time ago. The post is not about the spelling. It is about the ability of ff to give us clues and we don't even realize it. You have to pay attention if you are going to see them and they can come at you in really strange ways. I couldn't get this one. You would be on ground that is a bit more solid if you bought his book. Until then, thanks for stopping by.— r/ March 6, 2013.

Then the cavalry showed up (There were several like this).

In reply to ERM

YOU are missing the point...if you weren't so quick to judge, you would know that THEY AREN'T ARTIFACTS, FORREST USED TO HAVE A FOUNDRY AND HE HAD 12 BELLS MADE TO HIDE HIS MEMOIR IN! ... Do yourself a favor and go to the LIBRARY and do some research of your own, and quit being such a D#%8A$$. — ch&ss. February 28, 2013.

And then ERM replied:

hey look, sorry for jumping the gun, i didn't realize that "FF", whoever he is, made these artifacts, you're right i don't have no book, i honestly had never even, heard of this "story" (read TALL TALE) existed until i found this blog i found it on a search page for 'snark hunting', seriously, i just kept reading and got bewildered about your comparisons of misspellings, my apologies, hope y'll find what you're lookin for. — ERM. February 28, 2013.

With this, ERM became a treasure hunter, made several friends in the blog's commentary community and participated with gusto. Others? Not so much.

For example, here is one by Larson E. Whipsnade who used a name not his own and who probably didn't have permission to do so. His rather ungraceful comment was in response to one of my early posts that described Forrest in all his awesomeness.

Amateur archeologist my ass. Grave robber is more like it. By his own admission between those 321 missions in Vietnam he searched for and collected 'artifacts,' which he undoubtedly sold. What those were is not hard to guess since the country was full of bombed temples, buddhist monasteries, schools, museums, grave yards and homes. The Buddhists worship their ancestors and graves abound in status and artifacts left for the dead. Need it be mentioned that pillaging and looting in times of war is an international crime? When Fenn returned from the war he had enough money to move to Santa Fe and buy a gallery on Paseo de Peralta at the foot of Canyon Road, a pricy bit of real estate for sure. From the gallery he made a good deal of money selling Indian artifacts which everyone in Santa Fe knew were unearthed and taken from numerous un-excavated sites in Northern New Mexico. Those artifacts by law belong to either the Indian tribes and pueblos that are the descendants of the peoples who made them, or the State of New Mexico which has legal rights to any artifacts found in the state. So what he really was a grave-robber. — L.E. Whipsnade. March 11, 2013

Dear Mr. Whipsnade.

Calm down, my man. You are about to have a heart attack or a hernia and I don't want my blog to be the cause of it. If you pay attention, and obviously you don't, you would know that the FBI has closed its investigation and has apologized to Forrest for what they put him through. If you are something close to rational, I'm sure that you will do the same. r/ — March 11, 2013

What are You Willing to Give Up? This one shows the true dedication of a true believer. He talks of the large white blaze (the blazy-blaze) on a cliff face just downstream from Hebgen Dam and across the Madison River from the Campfire Lodge Resort.

> Richard, I just ran across your blog even though I have been on the search for a few years now. Last summer I found this blaze [below Hebgen dam] on my own. I managed to get to the other side of the river and search the area directly below the blaze. Alone in the area with the exception of a lone fisherman, I made it across with considerable effort but alas my shorts did not and so I found myself on the far shore standing tall in nothing but my birthday suit. I searched the boulders and mountainside buck naked for an hour, thankfully out of sight from all but God's creatures including a couple squirrels that didn't seem to mind the company. The swim back seemed easier and thankfully the lone fisherman had moved farther downstream thus sparing me a George Constanza moment. I wonder if you have searched the area yourself? — November 4, 2018.

Team Sleuthy-Guy was there twice, but mostly for the pancakes at the Campfire Lodge Resort. Given the image you leave me with, however, we may never go back. We did cross the river but if you didn't use a low center of gravity, it was 'no place for the meek.' Those who tried to walk it upright were soon on their keister(s) which made the crossing much easier.

Halloween: Now a comment with some fascinating information added to the post on "What is the Value of a Fenn?"

The value of a Fenn isn't always obvious to those who have not taken the time to learn about one. Fenns may appear to have more value when they are drained and their contents laid bare but those who have tended the fenns and have lived next to them for generations know better. Its mysterious nature may stir the imagination and stories told to warn the unsuspecting traveler away from the danger in the marshes. 'Beware the fen-fire,' some may whisper, the strange lights that flicker above the fenn-lands at night. Many have lost their way and never returned when lured into the fenn by the will o' the wisp, also known as a Jack O' lantern. But all things that appear mysterious have had legends grown around them. Trust those that know them. Trust those that know the fenns well for that is where their surname derives. These are the ones who can attest to a fenn's value. — Cloudcover. November 5, 2012.

"Can't, Can't, Can't" "Can't get there to find the box," seemed to be a steady refrain.

I believe I know where the treasure is placed. I think many of you are overthinking some aspects of this. FF is a man of honesty, but as my grandfather used to say. Don't tell them to much. So FF has given many clues. I think, I have figured them out, But I can't get there to find the box. I will say to all in this quest, you must look at how he speaks. A lot of ya'll are interpreting what you think he said. But not what he said. For example. 300 miles west of Toledo means that. But how can that be, that puts you in Wisconsin I think, One must think outside the box, as it were. I have the spot nailed down to about 1/4 mile radius. Actually, it's about a 250 foot circle. His clues make perfect sense to me. Weird, but I think I got it. So we'll be planning a vacation for next summer. — October 13, 2015.

So you went out to pick up the treasure during the summer of 2016 but didn't find it? Sorry. But you can take solace in the fact that 2016 was a bad year for everybody.

My Favorite: And last, my favorite. After I wrote the post 'What do Tom Fitzpatrick, E. Jean Carroll and Forrest Fenn Have in Common' I got this from Ms. Carroll:

> You are a brilliant man! The Appalachian Trail runs right behind my cabin.
> Let's go for a hike!
> Ravishing regards,
>
> E. Jean,
> March 26, 2012

I would love to go for a hike. I've walked about 150 yards of the Appalachian Trail and it seemed very nice. But wouldn't your ginger snap habit and my addiction to Oreos create unfortunate control issues along the way?

And the Hunt Trophy goes to . . .

Michael Hendrickson: poet, writer, quoter of quotes, connoisseur of all things Jemez, lover of country roads, lover of dance, lover of dogs, lover of people, lover of life, evader of death, baby-sitter, rider of motorcycles. I have never seen nor have I heard of anybody as positive about life as Michael.

Nor do I know of anyone with more bad luck. In just the short while we were on the blog together he lost his father and his best friend on the same day because they were the same person. He walked barefooted in a stream that led to an infection of his foot and the amputation of his lower leg; he was run off the road while riding his motorcycle by a hit and run driver, he was scammed by a homeless person he tried to help; his prosthesis fell off at least twice while riding down the highway on his hog, and he was always getting stuck in sand, mud, or snow because he did not understand the meaning of 'Don't go there.'

But he didn't hear that phrase from me because there is an abundance of sand, mud, and snow out there and, on his own, Michael will conquer more than his share of it.

Michael commented often on the blog where he gave us his treasure related adventures and spent whole pages telling us of the beauty he found around him while out there.

I wanted everyone to find Forrest's trove, of course, but most of all I wanted it to rest in Michael's storage shed.

CHAPTER 8

Heroism

Introduction: I took a long hiatus from *Mountain Walk*. There were reasons I did so and a confession seems necessary before I go. It was a conscious decision to take a breather and this is why:

First, In late 2015 a good bit of hate began to appear — not just in general across our country but also on the pages and blogs of Forrest's treasure hunters — just the opposite of what Forrest meant to do and certainly not what I had signed on for.

Second, far, far too many novices looked at Forrest's poem in a magazine, slept for a while, awoke and knew exactly where the treasure was located . . . yet they had no idea.

Third, as a result, it began to look as if the search community had been invaded by battalions of habitual gamblers who kept guessing wrong and losing. They didn't enjoy the search because they only wanted the 'get' and if they didn't get the 'get,' it was because the system was somehow rigged.

And fourth, people died while they searched for the treasure and I wasn't about to tell their families — especially their children — what was obvious at the time: that they had no real plan and thus were totally unprepared to do what they wanted to do. Like a great many who die each year on our public lands, they took little water, less food and no shelter; and the equipment some did carry proved useless. They didn't consider the weather they were headed into, and they had no idea of the idiosyncrasies of western rivers.

They paid little or no attention to what Forrest had said, "If your idea includes danger to yourself or to others, find a different idea."

This fourth 'why' is the main reason I decided to let the blog slide for a time but time moves faster than I once believed. The treasure was found and it had been over five years since my last post — the reason being that I had asked a question that my brain refused to answer:

If I could not explain that danger is always close for any real adventure, then how could I write a blog about what was, for many, a real adventure and then not deal with any of the deaths that came with it?

I hope I can do that now.

Mother Nature can be harsh. But, it would do little good here to cite the number of deaths just in the United States caused by natural phenomena that the weather channels tell us about: hurricanes, tornados, wildfires, icy roads, floods, tsunamis, etc. And, according to many, mistakes of all kinds, accidents that show without warning, and greed make these events even more tragic.

What does this say about the five and maybe six or more deaths among the 300,000 plus individuals who responded to Forrest's invitation to adventure? I will try to take on just two of them that, for me, were close to home: Randy Bilyou, and Brian Skilinski: Randy because he was in a place I knew well, and Brian because it was at a place where I then worked.

It wasn't greed that brought them down. Randy already had plans as to how the treasure would be shared if he found it; and Brian only wanted a very difficult physical and mental test to find himself. Though Randy was certainly looking for Forrest's treasure, there has been no official recognition that Brian was doing so. And, though Brian died high on a mountain side in South-Western Colorado and Randy died at the edge of a reservoir in Northern New Mexico, I see little difference between what both Brian and Randy were doing. At least for me, that means that both of them died as heroes.

The Problem of Naming Heroes: Of course I know that we cannot agree on just what a hero is. Joe Long is a friend who, when he retired as a commercial photographer, renewed his interest in fine art photography. I don't know what he called things in New York City, but now, when he takes a photo that has been perfectly lighted, composed, framed and the subject turns out to be an excellent choice, he calls that photo a 'hero.'

At the other end of my scale is a friend I had in high school in Los Alamos. His name was Guy Hodgkins and he was everybody else's friend as well — one of those who always smiled, who always helped, and who always had great ideas for the greater good. Foremost among his ideas was that, unlike the rest of us, he didn't want to go to college. He wanted to be a Marine. And so, when he graduated, the first thing he did was to volunteer.

I lost track of him for almost sixty years and only found him by chance when I read his name on a wall — the black one in Washington, D. C. that lists all 58,281[63] United States military men and women who died in Vietnam.

Guy had worked hard, as everyone knew he would, and became a platoon sergeant. Then, on one horrible day in that horrible war, a squad he led was ambushed and pinned down by two machine guns. Three of his men died in the first encounter. Almost immediately Guy charged the emplacements with a grenade in

---

[63] As of 2021.

each hand. He took out one machine gun and severely damaged the other before he died. For that he earned the Navy Cross — the second highest military honor of our nation.

Despite the confusion that surrounds current overuse of the word 'hero,' there is a standard definition used by the film and t.v. industries and that is accepted by many scholars.

The noted mythologist, Joseph Campbell, looked at the hero myths of a large number of cultures from tribes to nations to see what they had in common and discovered what he called the 'Hero's Journey' (Campbell, 1949). There appear to be a dozen or so commonalities that together are called the 'Monomyth.' It works like this:

For any future hero, there are two worlds: the ordinary world where he or she now resides and the special world where the journey will take place. The journey begins with a 'Call to Adventure'; that is, a call for the individual to cross a threshold and enter a special world of risks, dangers and the very real possibility that the journey could end in failure and its objective never secured. It is a very scary place.

During the journey, the hero meets a 'mentor' — a source of information and support during times of fear and resource scarcity. The hero also encounters enemies of various sorts and trials of all kinds, and must then engage in a final battle to secure the mission and win the reward that is then taken back to the normal world for the benefit of those who are from that place. If it happens that the hero dies during the ordeal, there is a resurrection and the hero becomes even more heroic.

Now, if the Monomyth carries the day and such a journey does, indeed, define a 'hero,' then neither Joe's very best photographs nor Guy's courage in battle would be considered 'heroic.'

Nor would any of the 58,280 other names on that dark wall in Washington mean anything in terms of heroism.

The Monomyth v Heroism: Obviously, something is wrong and it is this: the Monomyth is just that — a myth. Of course, a myth may or may not be 'true.' Myths do hold cultures together, they provide support to individuals in times of crisis; they can bring forth a sense of wonder and cement the ideas of community and of a common heritage. And, the Monomyth does hold within it truths about the hero's journey.

I suppose that a 'hero myth' must be that way and do what it does, but 'hero reality' is different; it is another view of heroism though the two begin in the same way. For both, there is a 'call to adventure' for the good of a specific and special people and once a threshold into that particular world of danger is crossed, the journey becomes evermore threatening. The call can come from anywhere — even from the hero himself or herself.

It is the positive response to that call and a loyal, even sacrificial, performance in the battles that ensue that make the hero a hero and little else. Yes, there may be a mentor, and there will be enemies of all kinds; there may even be a prize. But it is the response to that call that makes the hero and not a successful result of the effort. The hero must leave family and friends and all that is familiar and do it without knowing if the battles to be faced will be won or lost but certainly with a knowledge that survival is not guaranteed. Here is an example:

In May, 2016 my wife and I were volunteers in Great Sand Dunes National Park and Preserve in Southwestern Colorado; on the edge of the San Luis Valley. The part of the Park that holds the visitor center, most of the campgrounds, and the dunes themselves is at a high elevation — two thousand feet above the mile-high city of Denver (Anon, 2021).

Furthermore, the Preserve encompasses a portion of the Sangre de Cristo Mountain Range with half a dozen peaks of more than 14,000 feet and a whole lot of wilderness in between. Additionally, the San Luis Valley is often the coldest place in the lower 48 on any given day in any given winter and, though snowfall barely reaches 40 inches a year, it can come at any time between early fall and late spring.

As a part of my assignment, I sat on a stump in mid-May in the Park's lower campground and tried to convince a member of the Denver Police Department and his ten year-old son that they couldn't fly their drone in a national park. The 'whys' that normally come from a ten-year old now came from the forty-year old.

I tried a couple of reasons but he wouldn't agree until I said, "The air space over a national park is the national park's air space. It's a safety issue."

Before he could respond to that one, the 'whop, whop, whop' of a helicopter approached. It came in about sixty feet directly over our heads and landed in the parking lot.

Now, fully able to understand the rationale for the 'no drone' policy, he asked, "What is that about?" I answered that,

> Half of Southwestern Colorado is looking for a missing hiker. After last week's snowstorm, a ranger found a car that was not registered to be in the park overnight. When they figured out who it belonged to, they started a very intensive search: airplanes, helicopters, horseback, on foot, with dogs. The reason the downed tree limbs from the storm haven't been picked up is that the maintenance crew is trying to open the Medano Pass Road so that more ground searchers can get up there.

Brian Zelinski: They were all looking for Brian Zelinski, a forty-something year-old resident of Phoenix, New York (Anon, 2017). Brian's mother said that he had, "Gone out West for about a week." His friends said that he was going through a mid-life crisis and wanted, "A really difficult challenge to get himself back on track." The rangers at Great Sand Dunes said, "We have heard it all before."

Brian was not a stranger to Great Sand Dunes. He got what he wanted — twice. Earlier, in mid-February, he had taken a flight from New York to Denver, rented a car and drove to Great Sand Dunes. He was totally unprepared for what was before him. First, Phoenix, N.Y. has an elevation that is below 400 feet while the part of Colorado he was headed into has elevations between 8,000 feet and 14,000 feet.

Second, he told no one in the Park what he was up to. Third, he carried no water, little food, and no shelter. He spent four days wandering the snow-covered sand dunes which, once among them, block off any view of the mountains that could be used to get oriented. On the first night he removed his wet boots. They froze as he sat in the cold and he was never able to get them on again. When the rangers found him he was dehydrated, frostbitten and somewhat delirious. He spent a few days in the hospital, a few more in a motel, then got in his rental, drove to Denver and flew back to New York.

Now, less than three months later, he was again missing in a snowstorm somewhere in Great Sand Dunes National Park and Preserve. After ten days of intensive search and deteriorating weather, the hunt was terminated.

Brian's body was found a month later by two hikers when they saw his blue parka peeking through the then receding snow. His remains were removed from an elevation of nearly 10,000 feet in an area not searched in May because weather conditions made it too dangerous to fly over, and too hazardous to enter from the ground.

This 'call to adventure' came from Brian himself.[64] He answered it though he knew the dangers, the risks and the possibility of death. It was a challenge he chose to take, though between the weather, the mistakes and, more than likely, an accident or two, Brian lost. There was no prize, and there was no return to the ordinary world.

Randy Bilyou: Randy Bilyou lived in Colorado but he was from Georgia by way of Florida. He was after the Fenn treasure and had moved west to be closer to the areas he wanted to search.

In mid-January he went south with his dog to search for the treasure in New Mexico. He had bought a raft and a wet-suit with a plan to raft the Rio Grande through White Rock Canyon to a cave he thought he had found and, for Randy, there was no doubt that this particular cave held the treasure.

He put in at Buckman — an old, now gone, railroad stop on the Rio Grande less than twenty miles west and a bit north of downtown Santa Fe, New Mexico. The errors he had made up to that point assured him of one thing and one thing only — like so many others, he was not about to find the treasure he looked for.

First, Mr. Fenn had said many times that the treasure was hidden in the Rocky Mountains. Randy was not in, nor was he headed for the Rocky Mountains.

Second, Mr. Fenn wrote that the treasure was hidden in the mountains over eight miles north of Santa Fe. The problem here, for those who believed the hiding place was near Santa Fe, was that Forrest never said what he meant by 'Santa Fe.' Was the trove over eight miles north of the geographic center of Santa Fe? The

---

[64] When rangers in the Park were asked what they thought Brian was doing, 1/3 said they didn't know, 1/3 said it was probably suicide, and 1/3 said he was after the Fenn treasure.

population center? The center of the Plaza? The northern limit of the city? The northern boundary of Santa Fe County? The Santa Fe Opera? The North edge of the Santa Fe zip code? A wrong decision here could mean a search being made miles from the actual treasure. But, all of this had nothing to do with Randy because he was going south instead of north when he shoved off into the Rio Grande.

Third, Mr. Fenn had stated many times that the treasure was not in a place where an 80 year-old cancer survivor could not go. But with all the mud and sand that make up the delta at the head of the Cochiti Reservoir where Randy was headed and all the tree trunks one needs to negotiate to get there, Randy was about to embark on a journey that had defeated men half his age.

I have thought a lot about Randy these last few years — about whether or not he had read *Mountain Walk*, and if it would have helped him if he had. Would he have taken food, water, a shelter and a fire starter even if he thought the search would last just for the afternoon?

I wondered what his plan was to get out of the canyon once he got into it. Unless he knew exactly where the very few trails are that lead out of the canyon, he would be past them before he knew they were there. Did he know of the rapids a bit below where he put in — rapids that could easily flip a small raft, or damage an oar? Did he realize how shallow the river gets just before it reaches the reservoir and how the sand bars that build up would force him to disembark and pull the raft forward or that he could maybe walk on some of the sand because it was frozen but that if he broke through, he would be up to his knees in 'quick sand' and, unless he knew how to escape, it would take hours and all of his energy just to get free? What was his plan after he reached a reservoir that surely had enough ice on it to stop a rubber raft but not enough to carry a man?

I talked to Forrest just after Randy went missing to see if there was anything I could do but since I was in bed with a couple of broken leg bones because of a mistake of my own, I could do nothing.

I do not know what Randy thought or didn't think about the adventure he was about to enter when he pushed off into the river but it had to be a bit frightening. Except for his dog, he was alone; he had been in the West long enough to know that people go missing, that unexpected bad weather while out-of-doors is always dangerous and that western rivers are terribly quirky things.

Yes, Randy made a lot of mistakes just as Brian made a lot of mistakes. I've made a great many of them also. But there is nothing in the reality of a hero's journey, as I see it, that says mistakes will not be made and there is nothing there that says the journey must be successful.

A hero is defined in a multitude of ways but most all of the definitions include these things: (1) an affirmative answer to a call to adventure, (2) a separation from the hero's family, friends and home, (3) an awareness that the journey will entail risks of both mental and physical suffering that can include death, and (4) a journey that the hero was not totally prepared to make. The adult lives of both Brian and Randy fit very well within this schema of heroism. There is no reason to think of them as anything less.

CHAPTER 9

The Final Solve from Team Sleuthy-Guy

For any of you who want to take a trip out west for any length of time and spend some of it on the ground walking, hiking, camping, searching, climbing, thinking, looking or just being, I recommend you go to a library or a good bookstore before you leave home and that you hang out in two sections: Wilderness Safety and Geomorphology. The first is to ensure that you come back from your trip and the second is so that you max out your enjoyment of that trip.

What one needs to be safe outdoors has changed somewhat over the last few years and the main reason for this change is the smartphone. Of course there are some basics of survival that will never change; while you are in a wilderness a smart phone won't start a fire, keep you fed, hydrated, dry or from falling off a cliff and you will still need to tell someone where you are going and when you will be back before you lose the nearest tower signal. And, since a dead phone won't make enough noise to tell others when you are in trouble, you will still need your whistle.

However, if yours is a really smart, smart phone, you will have a flashlight, a camera, a magnifier, a GPS and maps; an empty notebook and keyboard, a compass and, if matched to someone else, it will tell them where you are. You can have a library and all of the information you will ever need if you download it before you leave. A charge of the battery will keep you afloat for a while but you can stay even longer if you carry a small portable solar charger along with you.

The West is way more fun if you can interpret the landscapes as you pass through them. Would you like to know, for example, what puts the colors red, green and black plus yellow, gray, pink and purple in all those rocks? Or know just why some of them are rounded and some are angular? You would even be able to tell if a glacier had wriggled by exactly where you stand some twelve to thirty-thousand years ago.

If you pay attention to your new geomorphology book, you will be able to say what caused all of those cliffs that people fall off of. You will know why the place looks like God had attempted a layer cake. You will know for sure that the spot you are standing on, all high and dry, was once under thousands of feet of sea water.

Do you want to find a fossil while you are out there? Then you, as a nascent geomorphologist, can do that and no one will need to tell you the difference between granite, limestone and basalt. More importantly, for now, and even more, more importantly, for then, you could have used your new-found understanding of geomorphology to help you find Forrest's treasure or, at least, it would have kept you east of the Rio Grande Rift as opposed to going all the way to the village of Cuba or clambering around the basalt boulders in the Box.

Better, you would have been able to explain to your fellow hunters why anything in New Mexico west of the Rio Grande and south of the Chama River is not in the Rocky Mountains. Which begs a question; how many of you searched the Chama River Basin and the Jemez Mountains absolutely certain you were about to stumble upon the treasure and you weren't even in the correct mountain range?

If you still want to find for yourself just where the treasure was hidden, Forrest told us that his clues were simple; so simple in fact that a child could find the treasure. But neither you nor I nor any other of the searchers are children and because of our ages, and the encrustations gathered around all of our senses, we will need a bit more clarity on what the clues tell us in these four areas:

Definitions: Forrest warned us about this one and the warnings are clear even if the words he uses are not. He will use his own dictionary, a vernacular dictionary, and not the one used by essayists to prove a point or by an attorney to win an argument. He also uses poetry where a 'sense' of the word is there even though a definition is not.

Scale: When Forrest says, "Look quickly down," does he mean for us to look down six feet to the base of a tree? Sixty feet to the bottom of a cliff? Two thousand feet along the length of an avalanche? Is the entire space covered by the set of clues a hundred sq. miles (2 miles x 50 miles)? Two hundred sq. miles (10 miles x 20 miles)? A thousand (an area with close to 32 miles on each side)?

Direction: Let's say that once you have chosen a point of departure, you then must choose a direction to go in. There are lots of directions to choose from but keep it simple and say there are but 360 of them. That's still a whole bunch, but Forrest immediately cuts that number in half when he says, "…canyon down." And he cuts it even further when he says that among those 180 different directions, you should choose just one — the one that your chosen canyon points towards.

Distance: The post, 'You had a Good Home but you Left,' left a number of *Mountain Walk* readers questioning my sanity and I got a lot of flak from some of you who thought that what I said was that you had to walk the 20-50 miles down a canyon full of rapids, large boulders, deep holes and man-eating *Bufo*s to get to where Forrest left his treasure.

But that is not what Forrest did and there was no need for us to do it either. He was 80 years old and could barely walk. So why do you think that you would have to make that trip? What I said, if I heard myself correctly, was that you should take the next step (Put in below the Home of Brown) when you are at a point twenty to fifty miles down that canyon and it does't matter how you got there or the route you took to get there. Take a car like he did and if a road crosses the canyon you are interested in at that point, take it as well. You don't need a helicopter or even a stabilizing line, let alone a rope that could maybe help you rappel down a cliff face.

Permanence: If I had to guess I would say that the 'clue' in Forrest's poem that most confounded most searchers for the most time was that of the 'blaze.' My view is that the blaze should be as permanent as possible. However, as an old on and off ecologist, the concept of change, and, therefore, of permanence, has always fascinated me.

Change is what ecology is about because change is so ubiquitous and important in nature and this is obviously so when the subject is 'blaze.' Virtually all natural processes will work to tear down any blaze we may want to create, form or fashion or that we may have chosen from a large number of natural possibilities. Finding a blaze that will last a thousand years — as Forrest seems to have wanted — would be difficult but that, it seems to me, is what we needed to do. In my mind Forrest's plan would only work if the 'blaze' in question were something that would last a long, long time.

Given all of this, here is a description of Team Sleuthy-Guy's first real 'solve' which centered in Montana from just below Earthquake Lake on the Madison River to its confluence with its West Fork. It was mid-August, 2013.

Somewhere in Montana:[65] Forrest has said that no one will ever just 'stumble upon' his treasure. To find it, one must actively look for it. He doesn't know my lovely wife.

Out tending to her life list of bird sightings (while the rest of Team Sleuthy-Guy looked for Forrest's treasure) she made a fascinating discovery and wanted everybody to know about it. First she found Biggie-Sleuth and Mini-Sleuth napping by a burbling brook.

Then she met Beat-Man and BKE who were seated on the step of an ancient abandoned cabin discussing the comparative influence of Camus and Seinfeld on the modern arts — music and film in particular, and repeated her story.

A bit later, she crossed paths with Mama-Girl who was wondering if any of us had been eaten by a bear and told her. Mama-Girl then found me as I happily skipped stones on the placid waters of a long skinny lake.

When I was told what my lovely wife had found, I said, "Where?" and as we walked along gathering stray members of

---

[65] MtnWlk Aug/22/2013

The Final Solve from Team Sleuthy-Guy

Team Sleuthy-Guy, I marveled at the fabulous landscape that Forrest's poetry had led us to: a short, narrow, incredibly serene valley with a stream full of trout and any number of fresh elk beds, piles of moose marbles and great heaps of bear-poo at least as tall as Poo-Bear himself.

Purple and yellow flowers bloomed everywhere and gave the whole scene a Van Gogh-ish glow. And, though it was mid-summer and we were just a short ten-minute walk from the road, we were entirely alone. It was mesmerizing and all of us decided that when it was time, there were a whole lot of grounds where 'our bones could rest forever' that were worse than the place we were in.

After a stroll of an eighth of a mile, we came upon the shaded edge of a meadow with a half dozen super-sized boulders.

Here, a small but important clarification needs to be made. It's no secret that my wife loves dogs, cats, birds, and horses as well as spiders, lizards and me — sometimes in that order. She calls us all 'Sweetie,' so when I saw what she had discovered I said, "Wow! This must be it!" and she said, "What?" And I said, "Forrest's blaze!" But she had only seen the pile of stones and the small sign below that misplaced chunk of limestone that says, "SHELBY" and then, "Every man should have one good dog in his life. I've had mine."

How she completely missed the graffiti on the 6' x 6' x 6' block of rock that reads, "Men Landed on the Moon July 20, 1969," was unusual since I had taught her everything I knew about both rocks and the clues of Forrest Fenn — and she missed them all!

Unsentimental fellow that I am, while everybody else lamented Shelby and his poor owner, I began to study the graffiti (Figure 11). It reminded me of a couple of things — one of which was the fact that a few astronauts had also been pilots in Vietnam and they may well have known Forrest Fenn.

Another was that this was the perfect Forrest Fenn blaze! What more could a pilot aspire to than to blaze a trail to the moon? Surely Forrest would be proud enough of the path blazed by his colleagues to note it on a rock! I took photographs and that evening I checked that writing against the handwriting found on pages 122 and 123 of his *Memoir* and this is what stared back at me (Figures 12, 13).

Figure 11: Graffiti, West Fork of the Madison River, Montana. "Men landed on the Moon July 20, 1969."

Figure 12: The letter 'J' Fenn *Memoir*.

Figure 13: The letter 'M' Fenn Memoir.

The lettering was at least similar and maybe identical! What is more, if you look 'quickly down' from that BLAZE, you see . . . Shelby . . .

However, being vegans and vegetarians who wave blood-filled mosquitoes off their arms and legs rather than smack 'em, there is no way that Team Sleuthy-Guy would ever let me dig up a dog for a mere one or two million dollars. Besides, I know who put the graffiti up there and it wasn't Forrest Fenn.

Doesn't mean he couldn't have used it as a blaze though; and there is nothing better than a ghost, real or imagined, to protect a secreted treasure.

So. How did we get to a spot that was so easy to get to; that was a perfect place for Forrest to hide his treasure, a place with a perfect blaze, just the right distance from 'warm waters halt,' and just below the 'Home of Brown' and yet fail to find anything? Here is the logic — failed though it be:

It starts with a belief that the treasure was never buried and that it especially wasn't buried in Yellowstone National Park because Forrest knew that it is illegal to bury anything in a national park.

Nor can you take out of a national park anything you may have dug up or even picked up in that national park.

Which meant that all of those thermal features within Yellowstone National Park were off limits. Besides, warm or hot springs occur throughout the West and there are 10,000 of them in Yellowstone National Park itself. How are you going to choose just one?

For us, the answer was, "You don't" and we felt this because the word "waters" is plural — it is the place where Forrest's poem becomes real poetry; the place where 'warm waters halt' is the border of Yellowstone National Park.

Next, you 'Take it in the canyon down.' But which canyon do you take it down? Yellowstone has more canyons than even I want to go into. And, because the Park covers not one but two calderas — the newer one inside the older and much larger one (well duh), the vast majority of the streams and rivers around and in, Yellowstone National Park flow into the park which means that none of those rivers would work.

The major exceptions that do flow out of the park are the Yellowstone River to the North, the North Fork of the Shoshone River and the Snake River to the South, the Belcher River to the Southwest (which soon puts it in Idaho), the Madison River to the West, and the Gallatin to the Northwest.

We chose to start with the Madison River for all kinds of good reasons one of which was that I had worked in Wyoming and had never been to Montana. Beyond that, West Yellowstone and the Madison River seemed to be where the Fenn family hung out during summer vacations.

For us 'Home' was not a boat launch; neither was it a ferry nor a mine. It had to be a Home. Therefor we interpreted 'Home of Brown' not just as a superlative for brown trout because of the capital B in the poem, but as 'Home of Brown' — a place where the brown trout are the largest or where you can find them in greatest numbers.

In Montana that is Wade Lake where the size record for brown trout for years was caught only to be superseded by the now record holder which was also caught in Wade Lake.

Wade Lake sits over a fault in a glacially carved valley fed by Lake Creek. The dam for the lake was naturally formed by a late terminal moraine of the glacier that originally helped carve the valley along an ancient fault line. Lake Creek flows for a mile or so below the moraine dam before it enters the small Smith Lake and then to the West Fork of the Madison River four or five miles further on.

If you want an adventure, walk a hundred yards or so of the creek just above its confluence with the West Fork of the Madison and you will find that there is no paddle up that one because as the small stream comes out of the forest it becomes a very mushy fen covered with a tangle of willows.

To find all of this, take US 287 from West Yellowstone and follow it west a little less than 50 river miles ('Not far but too far to walk') to where a bridge crosses the Madison River just below Earthquake Lake. Earthquake Lake was formed in 1959 when a large earthquake caused a landslide (heavy loads)[66] that put a dam across the Madison River (water high) making the slide scar a simple call as a blaze that is easy to find and that will last 'forever.' Keep left and that road will then take you up the West Fork of the Madison to a trailhead on the left with a Forest Service latrine and a small unimproved parking lot. Cross the 20 foot wide, ankle deep, West Fork, follow the trail to the left and you are in the

---

[66] 60,000,000 tons of rock and earth in one slide came down, dammed the Madison River, and went up the other side to create Earthquake Lake which then flooded and destroyed many summer homes just below Hebgen Dam.

valley we went into. Under this scenario, you have 'Put in below the Home of Brown' (Wade Lake).

It turns out, though, that all of this brings you to the wrong place because it is the home of the wrong Brown and we followed the wrong blaze along the wrong river, in the wrong state. But all of us agreed that it was an exceptionally fine vacation.

We had another river on the list to try, but Forrest, sly old codger that he was, of course knew we were on the wrong one and rather than hint that to be the case, he would casually give out a bit of interesting and true information that would keep us in the wrong place: "Campfire Lodge Resort? Ahh, yeah, I used to find arrowheads there."

It wasn't always comfortable being in the front row of this exercise of Forrest's: knowing him personally, writing a blog about the hunt, living in Santa Fe, having easy access to all his writings and interviews, getting his comments on *Mountain Walk*, and living Santa Fe's 'movable feast' of talk about the hunt. He knew what would have happened if any of his associates — as close as his grandson or as far away as yours truly, had found the treasure. It would have been complete chaos and more legal confrontations than there are now. I'm glad he kept me out of it.

However, after I learned that the treasure had been found in Wyoming and looked at a map a bit; it surprised me at how easy this could have been. The method Team Sleuthy-Guy had worked out for its first and only real hunt could have taken us straight to the treasure.[67]

Somewhere in Wyoming: When I decided to make something publishable out of *Mountain Walk* together with the idea that I could

---

[67] Of course, if he were asked if this is the real site, Jack could say, "Yes" or he could say, "No" and we still would not know if this is the site where the cache was cached.

now make sense of Forrest's poetry, it wasn't all merriment and bliss. There were reasons that Forrest and Jack Stuef, the finder, wanted the location of the hidden treasure to remain hidden. Given the off-chance that this solve is correct, did I want to be the one to go against their wishes?

Likewise, during my career, I often railed against the environmental non-profits when they sent reporters off to little known special parts of the world to write about how special they were only to then see those places trashed because of a newfound popularity. Did I want to be the 'reporter' here? Not really. But, there are also circumstances that tell me that, on this subject, I need to disagree.

Though I don't know Jack, Forrest was a generous, caring and well-intentioned friend who taught me something new every time I saw him and now there are those who want to steal his legacy.[68] That is, the naysayers are still here. They remain in the hunt with their heavy loads of negativity intact. Their declinations say that the whole thing was a hoax; that Forrest and Jack made a deal; that Forrest wanted his treasure back; that Jack didn't find the real treasure chest, that Forrest always tried to throw searchers off the trail when he saw that they were close; that he relocated the cache when he saw that they were getting too close; that his poem led searchers into dangerous places and the deaths belonged to him; that Forrest was a thief and a fraud; and then, that his poem meant nothing and that leads us once again to, "Its all a hoax."

Needless to say, I agree with none of this and the only way I could see to get rid of such nonsense was to use the poem and

---

[68] Anthony, 2020; Associated Press, 2021; Coombs, 2020; Goldberg, 2021; Vincent, 2021 among many others. See Bibliography for a larger sampling.

only the poem to find the place where Forrest's treasure had been hidden. And so, I will try.[69]

Again, we choose the boundary of Yellowstone National Park as the place 'where warm waters halt' (1) and then, we elect the Snake River as the 'canyon to go down' (2). This choice gives us the direction and the Snake River is the only accessible river of any size that comes out of Yellowstone National Park that goes into Wyoming without going almost immediately through private land. The North Fork of the Shoshone River also exits Yellowstone to the South as a small stream that gathers volume as it exits the Bridger-Teton National Forest, enters private land and then feeds into the Buffalo Bill Reservoir above Cody, Wyoming. The North Fork was enticing because of Forrest's relationship with that part of Wyoming but it lacked the neat packaging offered by the Snake River.

For example, if you go down the Snake River after it leaves Yellowstone National Park, you find that at a bit over 40 'too far to walk' (3) miles you are at its confluence with the Gros Ventre River, which possibly means that we are to, 'Put in below the 'Home of Brown' (4) if we can find a home of Brown in the area.

The 'solve' for this clue in Wyoming is different from that used in Montana. Brown trout in the Tetons is an invasive species and looked upon negatively. So we went elsewhere for the Home of Brown and found Grizzly 399 (The National Elk Preserve could also be used).

Grizzly 399 is the celebrated brown bear whose home range covers portions of Grand Teton National Park and the Bridger-Teton

---

[69] The poem from Forrest's *Memoir* is reproduced on page x. Here, the underlined phrases and the numbers indicate my choices for the nine clues from the poem.

National Forest around Jackson. Like '06,' the famous Yellowstone wolf, Grizzly 399 has a large coterie of photographers and admirers that follow her to the degree that she now has her own facebook page and Twitter account.

She was born in 1996 in the Bridger-Teton National Forest and was already famous in 2006 for her abilities as a mother and for her strategy of staying close to roads and settlements to keep her cubs from being slaughtered by the more elusive and malicious male bears.

Then, in June of 2007, an encounter with a hiker who surprised her and her cubs made her even more famous. She knocked him down, bit him on his back and buttocks and then left. The hiker told the authorities that he was the one at fault and they should not euthanize her — which is what normally happened after bear-human encounters. She is still producing cubs at the age of 26 and was recently photographed with four of them following along behind her (Balvin, 2021). One cannot find a better Home of Brown than that of Grizzly 399.[70]

<u>No paddle up your creek</u> (5). The Gros Ventre River between Lower Slide Lake and the Snake River remains filled with debris from the 1925 slide event and from the 1927 flood event which would make travel on the river difficult though possible. More to the point, however, is that 'paddling' is prohibited from the park boundary down to its confluence with the Snake River.[71]

---

[70] Grizzly 399 separated from her four cubs in May, 2022 and hooked up with a boar that had been following her. Now we just wait for the next group to come along.

[71] Paddling, which means rafting, kayaking, canoeing, and boating are locally prohibited in both Yellowstone and Grand Teton. In this case, it is the lower portion of the Gros Ventre River. Paddling is allowed from the Lower Slide Dam to the border of Teton National Park.

Figure 14: Scar of the 1925 Gros Ventre landslide. The flat area between the slide and small hills in the lower third of the image consists of debris from the slide.

Although, for some, the 'blaze' may be a clue, it does not need to be sequential; the poem does not say, "Now find the blaze." It says, "If you have been wise and found the blaze." A searcher should be able to discover the blaze soon after she or he put in below the Home of Brown since a relevant blaze would be something very large, close to permanent and easy to see (Figure 14).

This slide occurred during a period of heavy rain on already saturated soil which lubricated the discontinuity between a sandstone upper layer and the impervious limestone layer that makes up the base rock of the mountain where the slide originated.[72]

---

[72] For me, the 'blaze' is not a clue. The Rocky Mountains are young, steep, full of faults and they jiggle a lot (Thacker, 2017). Because of this, many hundreds, if not thousands, of major land slides have occurred in these mountains and their remnants are still visible (GeoWyo, n.d.). What this means to me is that one must not make a specific slide the first response in a search and then try to shoehorn everything else into that solution. A slide of this nature is flexible — it is not magic.

As the slide broke loose, it sent 50,000,000 tons of rock, soil, and trees down slope where it crossed the Gros Ventre River and went up the opposite slope for more than 300 feet. This debris created a dam a mile long and a half mile wide that brought forth Lower Slide Lake. Then, in 1927, the area once again received heavy rain on a heavy snowpack which caused the river to overtop and erode a portion of the dam. The resulting wall of water (50 feet high in some places) destroyed the town of Kelly roughly four miles downstream (Voight, 1978).

Heavy loads and Water High (6, 7). Fifty-million tons of debris is a heavy load and a fifty-foot wall of water appears to us to be a very, very high wall of water. Again, responses to these clues from the poem are seen in the debris from the Gros Ventre landslide and from the flood itself.

This material plus the river's relatively high energy level for much of the year, create class III and class IV rapids below the dam that make this reach of the river no place for the meek (8).[73]

In the Wood (9). The downslope area of the slide consists of talus, bits and pieces of forest that came down intact, a large number of logs and boulders and a relatively small forest that has regenerated over the last 96 years.

This clue appears to indicate that the search area is within one of these forested sections. Significantly, they are close to a road, close to local ranches and campgrounds, there is no water to wade through, they are a part of a National Forest rather than of a National Park and the area is as safe as you can get in the mountains of Western Wyoming.

---

[73] In May, 2022, a death by drowning occurred on this reach of the river when two men were thrown from their raft but only one of them was able to climb back on (Fike, 2022).

And that, using nothing but the clues from the poem, gives us an area the size of one or two football fields that could be defined as a 'search zone.' So, is this where Forrest hid and where Jack found the treasure? I don't know. What I do know is that all of this information is and was open, above board, and easy to find. Clues from the poem and only the poem were used to get us to this spot.

Any hints that Forrest passed along later in his interviews, writings or scrapbooks, were frou-frou and neither needed nor used to find what I believe to be the neighborhood of the cache. Given all of this, I am convinced that the cache was not buried except in the duff of the forest; it was not in a dangerous place; it wasn't moved until Jack moved it; and Forrest's challenge to us was not a hoax.

Not counting the four years that *Mountain Walk* was active, I spent less than a week on this solve. It all makes me suspect that the difference between Jack and most of the rest of us was little more than the difference between gumption and guesses. He found his place first and he did it on his own. We should respect it.

Within this search zone, the exact location of the cache would have been far enough away from the river bank and lake shore to be hidden from fisherfolk. As well, it would have been far enough from parking, trails and trailheads to keep the hikers and hunters away.

There are other ways to further define the search area. First, we can think of Forrest himself. Those of you who are near 80 years old or who watched your parents or grandparents as they aged, know that two walks to hide 42 pounds of stuff would be on the order of a half mile max each way. Only with great difficulty could Forrest have walked more than a total of two miles.

Likewise, an elevation change of a thousand feet would be 900 feet more than Forrest could have managed. Nor could he have carried a shovel or a pick in addition to the chest, made it across loose talus on a hillside, fought through a tight web of sagebrush, climbed over boulders and downed timber or even ventured into a tangle of pine or spruce.

The second is to use the words of Ms. Davis, formerly the Chief Ranger of Yellowstone National Park who, after discussions with both Forrest and Jack, said that she had seen the site and indicated that, "…the location is owned by the U. S. government and managed by the Department of the Interior" (Frick-Wright, 2022).[74]

Now, Mr. Frick-Wright's stories often have me on the edge of my seat, and I admit that I scooted forward a bit on this one. But, am I that far off? Or, can both be true? That is, can it be that the site is on Forest Service Land but "managed" by the Department of the Interior?

Well,…no, not really; by which I mean that the statement of Ms. Davis needs some adjustment to reflect what may be the actual case or, like thousands of others, I have gone down a fascinating rabbit hole full of promise, beauty and wonderment but little else.

I say this because the statement by Ranger Davis looks exactly like a Fenn head-fake, which suggests that a bit of due diligence is needed. And, what that extra bit of sleuthing shows is that the statement is 'correct' to a degree but not in the sense that it implies. That is, the Department of the Interior does not "manage land."

---

[74] Yes, I know of the 'debate' occasioned by the legal suit of Mr. McCracken against the Fenn estate which says that not only was the cache hidden in Yellowstone National Park but that Mr. McCracken knows where in Yellowstone it was hidden before it was 'moved.' And, of course, many past pro-Yellowstone folk seem to agree and are back on the trail. Others remain dedicated to Northern New Mexico or to Montana and the arguments continue.

In the end, though, I'll go with the lower part of the Gros Ventre slide in the Bridger-Teton National Forest as the site where the treasure was hidden.

Management activities on lands owned by the Federal Government can be under the jurisdiction of the Department of the Interior, but management activities are performed by the Department's services or bureaus (Bureau of Land Management, National Park Service, US Fish and Wildlife Service, Bureau of Indian Affairs and Bureau of Reclamation).

And the same is true for the Department of Agriculture and the lands under its jurisdiction where the Forest Service and the Natural Resources Conservation Service have land management portfolios.

The Department of the Interior would never assume to manage land under the jurisdiction of the Department of Agriculture and, of course, that is a potential 'problem' with this solve.

And, indeed, there are statements in the 'Wild and Scenic Rivers' legislation and some management plans that could lead one to believe that the Department of the Interior manages lands under the *jurisdiction* of the Department of Agriculture.

For example, the Gros Ventre River has a 'Scenic River' designation given by Congress in 1968 because of its 'outstandingly remarkable' values (Congress of the united States, 1968). Four documents shed light on what this means:

- the *Wild and Scenic Rivers Act* of 1968 which gives such designation to rivers or portions of rivers that meet the criteria given by Congress;
- the *Craig Thomas Snake River Headwaters Legacy Act* of 2008 which updates the list of rivers in the National Wild and Scenic Rivers System;
- the *Snake River Headwaters: Comprehensive River Management Plan/Environmental Assessment* of 2013 by NPS/USFWS, and the

- *Snake River Headwaters: Comprehensive River Management Plan* of 2014 by the USFS.

The first of these names the National Park Service as the institution chosen by Congress to study the 'free flowing' rivers and portions of rivers of the United States in terms of their 'outstandingly remarkable' values and make recommendations for their inclusion in a 'National System of Wild and Scenic Rivers.' It was here that the Gros Ventre River received its designation as a Wild and Scenic River.

The second piece of legislation is specific for the headwaters of the Snake River in Wyoming. It also includes the Gros Ventre River and adds more uses for portions of the river such as rafting and kayaking. These activities were not allowed and are still not allowed on the sections of the river that pass through Gran Teton National Park or that border the National Elk Refuge.

The next two documents are the NPS/FWS and the FS management plans respectively. They were developed congruently with, and cooperatively between these institutions and use a number of the NPS management rules for the river and its quarter mile buffer along its right margin (regarding unapproved raft access points and unplanned trails).

When the National Wild and Scenic River System was established, the National Park Service was made the chair of the system-wide Coordinating Council and this model remains the practice for many Wild and Scenic Rivers that flow through or that border more than one federal agency.

The Scenic River portion of the Gros Ventre River is one of these and is managed by an agreement between the National Park Service, the U. S. Fish and Wildlife Service and the U. S. Forest Service, and the NPS is the Chair of the Interagency Wild and Scenic River Coordinating Council for the Gros Ventre

River. Further, there is a statement on page 69 of the NPS/FWS Management Strategy that says,

> The first tier of this comprehensive river management plan includes headwaters wide management strategies that would be applied across the entire wild and scenic river designation (administered by National Park Service or the US Fish and Wildlife Service).

Does this make this bit of Forest Service land something "Managed by the Department of the Interior?" Again, I don't know, but if it does, it is not in the sense of Ms. Davis' statement and we are back where we started although with additional information that may help us find the cache site.

Here we can use a Venn diagram (apologies to 'Fenn Diagram,' Waterhigh, n.d.) of three intersecting circles: forest, slide, and the scenic river designation — especially its buffer zone. Location of the chest would then be reduced to an area suggested by the three intersecting circles. On the ground, our interest would be a site that includes all three of these entities.

Third, I am even more confident of this solution because of other things Forrest let us in on. He added hints for all of us to see — 'above 5000 feet,' the scent of 'sagebrush and pine,' and 'Not in Utah or Idaho' for example (Stump, 2013). Another of these hints was in his response to a *Mountain Walk* post in which I questioned his counting abilities:

> Richard, you couldn't count the clues correctly even if the lights were on. But since you are so eager I'll give you some help. When you go out looking for the treasure chest in this weather please take a warm coat, a wool face mask,

sealskin muck-lucks and a pint of wodka, all to keep you warm. — ff December 11, 2011.

His advice would have helped any of us as early as 2011 but no one realized it until way too late. You see, the very best place in all of Wyoming for ice-fishing is Lower Slide Lake and the people who go there to fish in winter, use all the adornments and, I assume, the refreshments, he suggested.

What about Forrest's neighbor and the red, green and black teas involved in the Olga story (Fenn, 2010)? Following my self-imposed Guideline Number 2 (page 9) which says that things that didn't look right should be looked at some more, I insisted in several posts that these were clues. They may be.

For example, the geologic map for the region around Lower Slide Lake indicates a bright red shale formation, a green shale at the top and bottom of the Gros Ventre formation and a black shale from the Bear River Formation — the site of the origin of the Gros Ventre slide (Love, 1975; Voight, 1978).

One need not be a geomorphologist to see that the Gros Ventre slide could easily be a correct response to the supposed clues set within Forrest's story about Olga. Forrest may or may not have known the names of these formations. But one cannot deny that the presence of those colors indicate that the lower portion of the Gros Ventre slide may have held his treasure. You only have to look. The whole land-scape around Lower Slide Lake is rendered in red from the shale, green from the trees and open spaces and black from the shadows. To show you what I mean, let me introduce you to 'Wyoming Jones' — a photographer from the area whose images can be found at:

https://flickr.com/photos/wyojones/albums/72157631960792955

The photographs taken by Wyoming Jones show that those colors are much more than Olga's tea choices (Jones, 2021).[75]

Then there is that thing that still troubles any number of searchers — the colophon. I sat on the edge of the bed the morning after I had discovered all of the above and as I finally got my second sock to where it was supposed to be, it occurred to me that I hadn't even considered the now famous omegas at the back of Forrest's latest books.

In spite of that, an answer came to me before I got my boots on and it only adds another layer of security to my belief that this solve is as close as we will get unless Jack decides to divulge his secrets.[76]

Many of those fortunate enough to have traveled the Earth would say that this part of it is surely one of its most beautiful as well as one whose human and natural histories captivate all who pass through. Don't go there unless you mean to take care of it.

Forrest said that he would like his final rest to be near his hidden treasure. Given his impeccable taste, it has been my view that any potential site for his trove would have all of the above qualities — and this one does. It doesn't matter now that his bones may be found elsewhere. What matters for me is that this is where his spirit resides.

It makes me want to go there to experience one of earth's exceptional places. Then, when I come back home and I think of this place, I can celebrate the lives of Forrest and Peggy; watch them as they dance among the boulders; walk with Forrest as he hides his treasures and follow along as he recites the hokey poetry that invites all of us to his game.

---

[75] His photographs also show excellent views of the Gros Ventre slide.

[76] Check out the elk antler arches at the entryways to the central square in Jackson, Wyoming.

You now have my answers to the poem's instructions. Your answers may be different and that, in my mind, is fine. My wish is that your discovery is a place as magnificent as this one, that it fills you with energy and curiosity and that it shows you something about our world and your place in it. That is what Forrest wanted us to search for and find; he called it, "The Thrill of the chase."

Bibliography

Aldrich, M. J. 1986. "Tectonics of the Jemez Lineament in the Jemez Mountains and Rio Grande Rift." *Journal of Geophysical Research*. https://doi.org/10.1029/JB091iB02p01753. Accessed 6/16/14.

Anon. 1629. A Discoruse concerning the Drayning of Fennes. London. [Dawnpiper, n.d. dawnpiper.wordpress.com/landwords. Accessed 6/16/14.

Anon. n.d. americanwhitewater.org. Accessed 12/18/21.

Anon. 2017. "Man Who Died in Great Sand Dunes had Gotten Lost in Park." https://www.denverpost.com. Accessed 11/11/21.

Anon. 2021. "The Great Sand Dunes." https://alamosa.org. Accessed 12/21/21.

Anthony, Michael. 2020. The Solve: Finding Forrest Fenn's Fortune and Leaking the Lie That Endangered His Legacy. Independently Published.

Associated Press. 2021. "Forrest Fenn treasure hunt: Man who sparked pursuit retrieved own loot, lawsuit says." The Denver Post. July 5.

Balvin, G. 2021. "Grizzly Bear 399 & 4 Cubs" The Best of 2021 Wildlife Photography-Grand Teton Park/Jackson Hole. gregbalvin/YouTube. Accessed 12/15/21.

Barbarisi, Daniel. 2020. "The Man Who Found Forrest Fenn's Treasure." Outside. December 7..

Barbarisi, Daniel. 2021. Chasing the Thrill. Knopf. New York. 348 pp.

Bibliography

Baylor, Byrd. 1985. Everybody Needs a Rock. Aladdin. 32 pp.

Campbell, Joseph. 1949. The Hero with a Thousand Faces. 3rd Edition. 2008. New World Library. 414 pages.

Case Text. 2021. Raphoz v. Fenn. Jul. 16, 2021. 1:21-cv-00553-WJ-JFR.

Case Text. 2021. Coombs v. Fenn. Dec. 27, 2021. 1:21-cv-00806-WJ-LF.

Case Text. 2020. Erskine v. Fenn. May 26, 2020. 3:20-cv-08123-DMF.

Coombs, Terry. 2020. The Fenn Treasure Conspiracy and Taylor Swift. Independently Published. 215 pp.

Congress of the United States. 1968. "The National Wild and Scenic River System." (Public Law 90-542; 16 U.S.C. 1271.)

Congress of the United States. 2008. Craig Thomas Snake River Headwaters Legacy Act. Government Printing Office. Washington, D. C.

De Voto, Bernard. 1947. Across the Wide Missouri. Houghton Mifflin Company. Boston. 450 pages plus maps.

Diaz, Johnny. 2020. "Someone Found a Buried Treasure Hidden in the Rocky Mountains." The New York Times. June 8.

Fenn, Forrest. 2004. *The Secrets of San Lazaro Pueblo*. One Horse Land & Cattle Co. Santa Fe, NM. 326 pp.

Fenn, Forrest. 2007. Teepee Smoke. One Horse Land & Cattle Co. Santa Fe, NM. 169 pp.

Fenn, Forrest. 2010. *The Thrill of the Chase: a Memoir*. One Horse Land & Cattle Co. Santa Fe, NM. 147 pp.

Fenn, Forrest. 2013. Too Far to Walk. One Horse Land & Cattle Co. Santa Fe, NM. 263 pp.

Fike, Ellen. 2022. "Ohio Man Killed in Class IV Rapids on Gros Ventre River in Teton County."cowboystatedaily.com. Accessed 6/23/22.

GeoWyo. n.d. Lower Slide Lake, the Gros Ventre Dam and the Gros Ventre Slide, Wyoming. http://www.geowyo.com/gros-ventre-range-granite-hot-springs.html. Accessed 7/1/22.

Goldberg, Julia. 2021. "Lawsuit alleges Fenn kept his own treasure." The Santa Fe Reporter. July 6.

Gunterson, Hugh. 2008. "The legacy of Ed Grothus and the Black Hole." The Bulletin of the Atomic Scientists. December 8.

Haines, Aubrey L. (ed) 1955. Osborne Russell's Journal of a Trapper. University of Nebraska Press. Lincoln, Nebraska. 191 pages.

Huckel, Bruce B. and J. David Kilby. Eds. 2014. Clovis Caches: Recent Discoveries and New Research. University of New Mexico Press. Albuquerque. 185 pp.

Jones, Greg L. 2021. https://flickr.com/photos/wyojones/albums/72157631960792955 Accessed 12/15/21.

Julyan, Robert. 1996. *The Place Names of New Mexico.* University of New Mexico Press. Albuquerque. Page 347.

Kennedy, Barbara. 1984. "On Playfair's Law of Accordant Junctions." Earth Surface Processes and Landforms. Wiley. https://doi.org/10.1002/esp3290090207. Accessed 2/21/15.

Leacock, George. 1988. *The Mountain Men.* Lyons Press. 256 pages.

Levinson, Michael. 2020. "Forrest Fenn, who Enticed Thousands with Treasure Hunt Dies at 90." The New York Times. September 9.

Lopez, Barry. 1991. *The Rediscovery of North America.* University of Alabama Press. 64 pp.

Love, J.D. 1975. "Geologic map of Gros Ventre Junction Quadrangle, Teton County, Wyoming. Open File Report 75-334. Accessed 6/15/22.

McClintock, Grant. 2010. Flywater. Universe Pub. 224 pages.

Myers, John M. 1963. The Saga of Hugh Glass: pirate, Pawnee and mountain man. Little, Brown. Boston. 237 pages.

Mysoor, Alexandra. 2017. "The Science Behind Intuition And How You Can Use It To Get Ahead At Work." *Forbes.* Feb. 2.

Nichols, John and William Davis. 1979. *If Mountains Die.* Alfred A. Knopf. New York. Page 8.

National Park Service. n.d. El Morro Guidebook. www.nps.gov. Accessed 12/12/13.

Office of the State Historian. *A Mountain of Life.* Santa Fe, N.M. newmexicohistory.org/filedetails_docs.php?fileID=21246. Accessed 5/7/13.

Prince, L. Bradford. 1977. "Spanish Mission Churches of New Mexico." Rio Grande Press. 373 pages plus index.

Prokop, Danielle. 2020. "Hunt is Over, or is it?" Santa Fe New Mexican. Pressreader. Accessed 3/12/21.

Reddit, n.d. reddit.com r/FindingFennsGold;

r/Forrest Fenns Treasure. Accessed 5/12/21.

Sanches, Robert. 2016. "How One Colorado Man Disappeared While Hunting for Hidden Treasure." 5280. Denver's Mile High Magazine. August.

Science Encyclopedia. n.d. "Phototropism Research, Cholodny-Went Theory. JRank Articles. Accessed 1/12/14.

Stump, Scott. 2013. "The treasure is not hidden in Idaho or Utah." TODAY. June 28.

Thacker, Jacob. 2017. "Seismic Proportions" *Bozeman Outdoors.* Summer.

Tschirhart, John. 2009. Integrated Ecological-Economic Models. The Annual Review of Resource Economics. 28:28.1-28.27

United States National Park Service. 2013. Snake River Headwaters: Comprehensive River Management Plan/Environmental Assessment. Department of the Interior. Washington, D. C.

United States Forest Service. 2014. Snake River Headwaters: Comprehensive River Management Plan. Department of Agriculture. Washington D. C.

UnitedStates Forest service. n.d. https://www.rivers.gov/documents/plans/snake-headwaters-plan-usfs.pdf . Accessed 6/12/22.

Vigdor, Neil. 2020. "Man Who Found Hidden Treasure in the Rocky Mountains is Revealed." The New York Times. December 7.

Vincent, Isabel. 2021. "It Doesn't Make Sense: Mystery Still Surrounds Forrest Fenn's Treasure Find." New York Post. July 11.

Voight, Barry. 1978. "Lower Gros Ventre Slide, Wyoming, U.S.A." Developments in Geotechnical Engineering. Volume 14, Part A, Pages 113-162.

Waterhigh. n.d. https://thefenndiagrams.com. Accessed 12/18/21.

Went, F. W. 1945. Auxin, the Plant Growth Hormone II. The Botanical Review. 11:487-496.

Went, F.W. 1973. Competition Among PlantsProc. Nat. Acad. Sci. USA. Vol. 70, No. 2, pp. 585-590.

Wikitravel. n.d. "Jemez Mountains." Accessed 1/20/22.

Williams, Megan. 2017. "How O-six Became Yellowstone's Most Beloved Wolf". CBC Radio.

WINROCK INTERNATIONAL. 1984. A National Rangeland and Rain-fed Watershed Program. Hashemite Kingdom of Jordan. Team Member.

Worrall, Simon. ND. The 'Most Famous Wolf in the World.' Lived Hard — and Died Tragically. National; Geographic. http://nationalgeographic.com Accessed 6/22/20.

Acknowledgements

When I asked my high-school English teacher why an 'acknowledgment' section was necessary in a book, she said, "Think of it as a graduation party where all the graduates are there to celebrate the completion of their work and their support for one another. Its a party — enjoy it."

I must admit that it is rather interesting to remember things in that way. For example, it seems to me that anyone who is essentially a free bookstore, the author of the study book itself, the one who is the benefactor for the play we are in as well as its playwright, who can make fun of you when fun should be made of you, who is compassionate regarding the lives of others and passionate for what he does and wants you to be a part of it, then all of that should be acknowledged. Here I speak of Forrest Fenn and I do so.

Leslie Wray McBride and Henry Aragoncillo are friends from a few photography courses we took together. The three of us went out to find Waldo (a ghost town south of Santa Fe) along the railroad to photograph the abandoned coke ovens and decided that the next time we went to Waldo, we would get there early enough to 'moon' the AMTRAK as it came by.

Leslie is in this book because she is the one who introduced me to Forrest Fenn. Henry is in this book because he is the buddy I keep telling you to take along on your adventures. He, like me, at the drop of anything, will jump into my heirloom pickup and head for anywhere there is a more or less passable road to get there. Knowing northern New Mexico as we do is why I thought that many of the 'solves' that involved New Mexico were nonsense and it was all Henry's fault. I do, indeed, acknowledge both Leslie and Henry.

For keeping me grounded, Team Sleuthy-Guy, my 'discovery' team, deserves acknowledgements as well: Lovely Wife, Mama Girl, Biggie Sleuth, Minnie Sleuth, Beat Man and BKE all get acknowledged.

'Lovely Wife's' birth name is Gayle and she is the very person in my life who keeps me fed, clothed, clean, more or less sane and loved. Every time we went out to look for gold, she spent her time looking for birds. I'm sure she believes it worth the million dollars we didn't find.

'Mama Girl' (Teri Saunier) is a real daughter-in-law but far too young to be a mother except she is pretty much the best one I've ever seen. When we went out to look for gold she took a lot of photographs. It was a gorgeous place we were in.

'Beat Man' (Greg Saunier) and 'Biggie Sleuth' (David Saunier) were born as fully grown musicians. The first does rock with a band that has 25+ years under its belt and no day job. Like many other bands, the band has traveled the world but seen little of it. The second does a reggae thing in two or three bands around Baltimore when he is not designing stuff with and/or beside Teri. Both musicians deserve very high marks for their ability to focus — on everything but a hidden treasure of gold.

Rebecca James (BKE) is the son I never had. She rides horses, brands cattle, fishes for trout, ties her own flies, can wade any wadeable river in Yellowstone and teaches film animation at the New School in New York City. Slim at something like 5'9" and 130 pounds, she never met a Campfire Lodge Resort flapjack she couldn't handle. But gold? "Meh."

Minnie Sleuth (Aden Saunier) was about two years old when we were on the hunt and his self-imposed task for the week was

Acknowledgements

to dam the Madison River one pebble at a time. He often threw under-handed but forgot to establish his release point and the pebble would go straight up and then straight down to hit him on the head. Still throwing, he is now a pitcher with one of the local kid's teams and throwing strikeouts is his game.

Adele Levine and Richard Meganck also get acknowledged. I asked them to read this thing because it has now been 50+ years since they first felt a need to correct my grammar. Dr. Meganck lives somewhere in Oregon but it changes so often that I can't keep up. Ms. Levine has adopted the entire town of Bracket, Massachusetts and that includes a black bear and her cubs, several sugar maples and a local motorcycle gang.

Life is good when all of them are around and I would be irretrievably lost without them.

Four other groups should be named and acknowledged:

Google Earth because of how it changed everything from geography to spying to finding old expensive boxes full of gold;

GeoWyo, a small group of Wyoming geologists who have a remarkably informative website that should be used by anyone interested in finding a cache of gold in Wyoming as well as for learning the geomorphic history of the place; and

The web-site that taught me how to speak 'Old English' which is found at 'dawnpiper.com' and should be looked at by anybody interested in old stuff.

Ms. Dorothy Massey, of course, is not a group. She is the owner of the Collected Works Bookstore, and her smile accompanied every book of his that Forrest asked her to give me. This book store is the place in Santa Fe to visit: have a coffee, chat with a staff member, talk to a local, browse all the books you want, take a nap. Although you will come out of there with less money than you had when you went in, you will be far richer for it.

About the Author

Richard E. Saunier holds a PhD in Range Ecology and an MS in Watershed Management from the University of Arizona as well as a BS in Forestry from Colorado State University. He was Professor of Forest Ecology and Silviculture at the *Universidad Austral de Chile* in Valdivia, Chile, Deputy Director of the Peace Corps in Paraguay, and Regional Officer for Environmental Programs for the Peace Corps in Latin America and the Caribbean. After reaching the five year limit for employment as Peace Corps staff, he became the Senior Environmental Management Advisor at the Organization of American States. Now retired, he and his wife volunteer in the national parks of the Southwestern United States.

www.ingramcontent.com/pod-product-compliance
Lightning Source LLC
LaVergne TN
LVHW011827060526
838200LV00053B/3932